Reconciliation

Reconciliation
Our Greatest Challenge—Our Only Hope

Curtiss Paul DeYoung

Judson Press ® Valley Forge

Reconciliation: Our Greatest Challenge—Our Only Hope
© 1997 Judson Press, Valley Forge, PA 19482-0851

Bible quotations in this volume are from the New Revised Standard Version of the Bible, copyright © 1989 by the Division of Christian Education of the National Council of the Churches of Christ in the United States of America. Used by permission. All rights reserved.

Library of Congress Cataloging-in-Publication Data
DeYoung, Curtiss Paul.
  Reconciliation : our greatest challenge—our only hope / Curtiss Paul DeYoung.
  p. cm.
  Includes bibliographical references.
  ISBN 0-8170-1256-7 (pbk. : alk. paper)
  1. Reconciliation—Religious aspects—Christianity. 2. Sociology, Christian.
I. Title.
BT738.D48 1997
234'.5—dc21   96-49543

Printed in the U.S.A.
05 04 03 02 01 00 99 98 97
10 9 8 7 6 5 4 3 2 1

In gratitude to Calvin S. Morris,
my friend and mentor,
for helping me understand reconciliation as a process

In memory of Alexander Cordero (1943–1996),
my friend and co-laborer in the ministry of reconciliation

Contents

Foreword

This book appears at a crucial time in the life of America and the affairs of our world, for everywhere one looks, conflicts between persons and groups are playing themselves out, with evident and uncivil struggling over differences—differences in values, ethics, religious views, land claims, territorial rights, and a host of other fractious debates. Conflict holds center stage in our time, and voices of wisdom addressed to those involved in the fray—or to enlist persons of good will to help quell the conflicts—are all too few.

Curtiss Paul DeYoung is one of those voices, and this book is his attempt to share wisdom—a biblical wisdom tested in his own life struggles—with the rest of us. Addressing himself courageously to our hearts as well as our heads, DeYoung honestly treats reconciliation as the costly action that it is, and he explains the need for relational bridge building at the many levels of our social interaction. One of his most strategic sentences is this one: "What has cost God much cannot be cheap for us. Costly reconciliation is the Incarnation of God."

This book is a logical and planned sequel to the author's previous book, *Coming Together: The Bible's Message in an Age of Diversity*, which treated the Bible as a record of a culturally diverse people seeking God's will, and how the person Jesus—

"an Afro-Asiatic Galilean Jew"—became a universal Christ who liberates, shapes a new and inclusive community, and empowers his followers to be agents of reconciliation. The present book was written to "unpack" the meaning and scope of reconciliation, the call for which ended *Coming Together*.

The strength of this book is in the systematic considerations DeYoung has offered about how the shared life of "the community of the reconciled" contributes to the work of justice issues, a greater visible unity of believers, and positive social change. Christian faith is seen not only as intelligible but as productive and persuasive.

This is a book for which its author can be proudly accountable. There are places in it where he calls attention to how he came to know what he reports, and he reports it with a responsible bearing. What he has distilled from his depth study of the Christian Scriptures is also highlighted, with necessary mention of the relevant literature within the field of his topic. One values this holistic approach, the careful exposition of insights from his prolonged observation of the perennial needs of the church and the world. Some of the formulations voiced herein have been reshaped across the years, corrected or confirmed by interaction with other minds and lives, but the accent DeYoung places on the imperative for courage to work at reconciliation—"taking responsibility, seeking forgiveness, repairing the wrong, healing the soul, and creating a new way of relating"—is from a wisdom generated by his own serious faith and dedicated walk as a believing, teaching, active practitioner of *agape* love. Due reflection on what he has written here should lead not only to an informed understanding of what reconciliation means, but also to commitment of oneself to the risks it involves and the responsible action it demands.

This book was not narrowly conceived, nor is it selfishly motivated. Knowing Curtiss Paul DeYoung as I do (from across his college and seminary years on into his service in ministry), I know that this book reflects the honesty and hope that characterize his spirit. If read in the light of the author's intention for it, namely, to clarify our human possibilities and enhance our lives through the spirit and work of reconciling love, this book not only offers a necessary and timely statement but alert guidance by which to work at the most challenging and necessary task in our time: reconciliation. Here is guidance, based in a vital Christian faith, that is never past tense but is contemporary, focused, and creative.

James Earl Massey
Dean Emeritus and Distinguished Professor-at-Large
Anderson University School of Theology

Acknowledgments

I want to express my gratitude to many of the people who faithfully supported me in the process of writing this book. I first must thank my friend Perry Hunter for suggesting that I write this book. I want to declare my sincere appreciation for the support I have received, during the months of writing, from the staff and board of directors of TURN Leadership Foundation. Also many individuals in TURN's broad network of relationships in Minneapolis and St. Paul have encouraged me in significant ways.

I am deeply indebted to Robin Bell, William Huff, Aldean Miles, and Katherine Miles for reading the manuscript and offering affirmation and helpful suggestions. Their input made this a much stronger book. I also must thank Harold Rast and the staff at Judson Press for their support. Special thanks go to Kristy Arnesen Pullen and Mary M. Nicol for their strong encouragement.

I could not have written this book if many had not trod this path before me. Insights from the writings of Howard Thurman were especially beneficial. I felt the absence of my mentor Samuel Hines as I wrote this book, yet his example as Christ's reconciler remains fresh and empowering.

The first person on my journey in ministry who articulated and modeled for me the ministry of reconciliation was James

Earl Massey. He has been a mentor and guiding influence in my life for over twenty years. Words cannot adequately describe the formative impact he has had on my life. There is no person I would rather have write the foreword to this book. I am highly honored that Dr. Massey took time out from his very full life to accept my invitation.

This book could not have been completed without the generous understanding and endless support of my wife, Karen, my daughter, Rachel, and my son, Jonathan. I am deeply grateful for their love. I am very grateful to Karen for reading the manuscript and offering helpful insights and reassurance. I hope this book contributes to a better future for Rachel and Jonathan.

Finally, all praise and honor go to the most significant inspiration in my life—Jesus Christ, the reconciler par excellence!

Introduction

In the decade of the 1990s, reconciliation became big news in church life. The Southern Baptist Convention offered a public apology to African Americans for the involvement of Southern Baptists in slavery. Roman Catholic Pope John Paul II of Rome and Eastern Orthodox Ecumenical Patriarch Bartholomeos I of Constantinople came together for a service in Rome and offered a joint blessing. The pope also issued a letter of apology for the church's role in the oppression of women and called for the equality of the sexes. Billy Graham preached a sermon via satellite from San Juan, Puerto Rico, that was simultaneously translated into 116 languages to people in 185 countries in all 29 time zones. The church has also taken the lead in initiating many of the miraculous changes occurring in South Africa.

Several Christian organizations in the United States have issued a call for reconciliation. The National Black Evangelical Association and the predominantly white National Association of Evangelicals are seeking common ground. In 1994 the Pentecostal Fellowship of North America, which represented white Pentecostal denominations, disbanded and, in concert with African American Pentecostal denominations, formed a new racially inclusive organization, Pentecostal/Charismatic Churches of North America. Christians for

Biblical Equality, the Biblical Institute for Social Change, and the Reconciliation Initiative are examples of organizations lifting up the biblical mandate to be agents for reconciliation and justice. The Fellowship of Reconciliation has been working at reconciliation for over seventy-five years from an interfaith perspective. In addition, a number of organizations and movements have identified reconciliation as a part of their agenda: World Vision, Promise Keepers, the Council of Leadership Foundations, the Christian Community Development Association, Call to Renewal, and others. Several books on the subject have been published as well, and a number of the books on racial reconciliation have been co-authored by an African American male and a white male.[1]

This emphasis on relational bridge building has also been expressed on the local level in the form of congregational partnerships across the divide of city and suburb, race or denomination. Pulpit swaps, choir exchanges, unity services, reconciliation rallies, fudge-ripple sessions, dialogues, and marches have been held. Hundreds of training events and sensitivity sessions have been offered on topics like cultural diversity, gender equity, and antiracism.

What does all of this mean? Are we who claim to follow Jesus Christ moving toward a time of greater visible unity? Will issues of justice receive a higher priority and therefore make positive social change more of a reality? Or is reconciliation just the latest fad in Christendom? Is all this reconciliation talk merely more guilt-reducing rhetoric? Does the advent of Afrocentric and womanist perspectives among African Americans, and similar trends among other groups, actually lead to greater separation? Or are these responses to society's attempts at marginalization necessary preludes to genuine unity? These questions are crucial for our time. While we talk about reconciliation, our world is ripping at the seams because of hatred, violence, racism, classism, sexism, homophobia, nationalism, and anti-Semitism. Events like ethnic cleansing and urban street battles seem diametrically opposed to the forces of reconciliation, as do continuing problems like the domination of women and the corporate exploitation of the poor.

If we are honest, we will admit that even among those who claim to be followers of Jesus Christ we see evidence of the same divisions found in broader society. Furthermore, Christianity has its own unique brand of infighting and competition. Christendom's celebration of separation is easily observed in its denominationalism, where Protestants have become connoisseurs of fragmentation. So we return to the question: Is this talk of reconciliation merely today's fad, or is it directing us to the source of tomorrow's hope? This book, *Reconciliation: Our Greatest Challenge—Our Only Hope*, seeks to clarify what biblical reconciliation is and what precipitates it. Generations to come face dire consequences if we do not embrace a reconciliation that is life changing, society transforming, and long-lasting.

Sixty years ago a number of church leaders in Germany were being subtly seduced by the charisma of Adolf Hitler. It was the contention of Lutheran pastor and theologian Dietrich Bonhoeffer that many Christians were practicing a "cheap grace" that allowed them to be co-opted by the Nazis to support their ultranationalism and excessive bigotry. Bonhoeffer declared that cheap grace was "the preaching of forgiveness without requiring repentance . . . grace without the cross, grace without Jesus Christ, living and incarnate."[2] In 1937 Bonhoeffer published his book *The Cost of Discipleship* in a bold attempt to awaken a church that he felt was compromising the call of Christ. He challenged Christians to embrace a "costly grace":

> Costly grace is the gospel which must be *sought* again and again, the gift which must be *asked* for, the door at which a man must *knock*. Such grace is *costly* because it calls us to follow, and it is *grace* because it calls us to

> follow *Jesus Christ*. It is costly because it costs a man his
> life, and it is grace because it gives a man the only true
> life. . . . Above all, it is *costly* because it cost God the life
> of his Son: "ye were bought at a price," and what has
> cost God much cannot be cheap for us. Above all, it is
> *grace* because God did not reckon his Son too dear a
> price to pay for our life, but delivered him up for us.
> Costly grace is the Incarnation of God.[3]

Unfortunately, not enough people responded to Bonhoeffer's plea for costly grace. Cheap grace exacted a cost of its own: a defeated and divided Germany, a disillusioned church, the genocide of over 6 million Jews and others, and the loss of one of the church's brightest minds in the death of Bonhoeffer.

It is now 1997, sixty years since Dietrich Bonhoeffer published his treatise on costly grace. I am writing this book with the hope that, as we move into the next millennium, we will not settle for a cheap form of reconciliation but will embrace the understanding that true reconciliation is costly. Cheap reconciliation is unity without responsibility, forgiveness without repentance, equal treatment without restitution, harmony without liberation, conflict resolution without relational healing, peace without God.[4] I believe that the price of cheap reconciliation could be as devastating for our future as cheap grace was for Germany. This book challenges us to consider a costly reconciliation. When God, through grace, reconciled us, it came with a price, the crucifixion of God's son, Jesus Christ. *What has cost God much cannot be cheap for us. Costly reconciliation is the Incarnation of God.*

My approach to the study of reconciliation is a holistic one. I am troubled when I hear people speak with great clarity regarding racial reconciliation who are still locked into hierarchical views on gender issues. Some individuals work hard to eradicate class distinctions but are anti-Semitic. Others promote gender equality but do not include race and class in their critique of society. Such contradictions undermine otherwise commendable efforts toward unity and social justice. Sexism, classism, racism, and all other forms of bigotry are intertwined. Therefore, our attempts at breaking down walls should not be thought of as separate initiatives. We must have a comprehensive understanding of reconciliation before we can effectively focus on particular issues. Many of the same forces are at work in the multiple forms of discord that we encounter. Similar principles and processes are needed for creating greater harmony no matter which "ism" one seeks to address. Throughout this book I examine reconciliation in its broadest sense. Although my remarks are focused primarily on the need for reconciliation in the United States, I include examples and insights from around the globe and hope that my conclusions are applicable to settings outside the United States.

In part 1, "A Costly Problem," I identify the multiple barriers that block harmony in our world and offer numerous examples of the ways in which reconciliation is inhibited and undermined. We should not underestimate the complexity and depth of the fragmentation in our society. Yet it is easy to become overwhelmed and discouraged by the barriers and give up on the possibility of reconciliation. Be sure to read beyond the first three chapters!

The biblical mandate found in 2 Corinthians 5:18 provides us with perspective and hope: for God "reconciled us to himself through Christ, and has given us the ministry of reconciliation." Part 2, "A Costly Proclamation," begins with a chapter titled "God's One-Item Agenda." This chapter examines the meaning of the biblical word *reconciliation* in the contexts of the first century and today. The practice of Jesus and the early church, as it relates to the ministry of reconciliation, is also examined. In chapters 5 and 6, I outline some principles for guiding our attempts at pursuing togetherness.

Chapters 7, 8, and 9 describe the essential steps for actually engaging in the process of reconciliation: taking responsibility, seeking forgiveness, repairing the wrong, healing the soul, and creating a new way of relating. This part, "A Costly Process," is the core of the book. Both the invigorating challenge and the painful struggle involved in achieving the goal are acknowledged. Models that have encouraged hope in various settings are lifted up for consideration. The book's epilogue briefly examines the role of the reconciler and the cost of practicing reconciliation.

A brief comment is in order regarding the relationship of this book to my previous book, *Coming Together: The Bible's Message in an Age of Diversity.*[5] In *Coming Together* I looked at biblical interpretation through the prism of cultural perspectives and demonstrated that the Bible itself is the record of a culturally diverse people seeking God's will. I highlighted the consistent biblical call to oneness and the intentional inclusion of people who were marginalized by society and at times by the community of faith itself. I also demonstrated that an Afro-Asiatic Galilean Jew named Jesus became a universal Christ; that all people can hear their story in the Bible; and that the Bible witnesses against racism, sexism, and classism while speaking in favor of community, liberation, and empowerment. *Coming Together* ended with a call for reconciliation. While *Coming Together* provided a deeper biblical background for many of the themes addressed in the following pages, *Reconciliation* differs in focusing on the *process* needed for coming together at a time in history when we find ourselves so far apart. That process is found by unpacking the action-packed word—*reconciliation*.

The subject of this book is my life's passion. The unique way in which I interpret and understand reconciliation is a synthesis of all that I have observed and experienced in my nearly forty years. My childhood was spent in a family where the humanity of a person was more important than society's label. I was raised in the Church of God (Anderson, Indiana), a church that is theologically committed to unity. My adult identity began to take shape in New York City, where I simultaneously lived in a Catholic community that daily modeled for me radical Christian faith, worked with homeless young people in Times Square who "schooled me" with their painful life stories, and served in a Harlem congregation that nurtured me as a young minister. Further growth took place in Washington, D.C. There I studied with professors at Howard University School of Divinity who taught me to free my thinking from a Eurocentric bias; I interacted with homeless men and women who slept on the streets in the capital city of the most powerful nation in the world; and I was mentored by Samuel Hines, a true artisan of reconciliation.

My understanding of reconciliation has expanded during the 1990s. For five years I pastored a multiracial congregation in Minneapolis, Minnesota. At the request of a social service agency seeking to broaden its network in the faith community, I interviewed more than eighty religious leaders in Milwaukee, Wisconsin, from a wide range of religious traditions, cultures, languages, and races (this required me to shift relationally into a different cultural or religious perspective four or five times a day).[6] In writing *Coming Together* I studied the work of biblical scholars and theologians from widely diverse cultural perspectives (this caused me to experience cultural shifts intellectually). Currently I serve as the president of TURN Leadership Foundation, a multicultural urban ministry network that works for reconciliation and social justice in Minneapolis and St. Paul.

These experiences, the great tensions of our times, and my hearing of the biblical mandate to be a minister of reconciliation have compelled me to write this book. Writing *Reconciliation* has been a very personal journey, taking me along the path of vulnerability, self-analysis, and risk. My understanding of reconciliation is still far from complete, and the process has not always been clean and tidy. Because reconciliation is itself a process, this book may well have an "unfinished" feel. In fact, it is a work in progress. I simply hope that the book will provoke people of God to take the conversation about reconciliation to a deeper level. I also hope it will encourage people of faith to launch experiments in unity. It is at the roundtable of dialogue and in the laboratory of life that we truly discover how to move reconciliation from a rhetorical exercise to a realized experience. This book is penned as a clarion call to followers of Jesus to strive for a peaceful future. Reconciliation is our greatest challenge as we enter the twenty-first century—and it is our only hope!

Part I

A Costly Problem

1

The Dividing Walls

The 1990s have offered us the disillusioning opportunity to discover the degree to which the human family is fragmented. It is a disturbing revelation. The torturous acts of ethnic cleansing in the former Yugoslavia demonstrated how far people will go to preserve their own group identity at the expense of "the other." The assassination of Israeli leader Yitzak Rabin by a Jewish extremist displayed the extent to which, even within one's own group, an individual will go to protect a separatist theology. During the past few years in the United States, we have had to face the truth of our own hostility and separation. This has been best illustrated by the responses of people to courtroom verdicts in two cases.

The 1992 "not guilty" verdict in the trial of white Los Angeles police officers charged with severely beating Rodney King, an African American, provided us with a glimpse of the depth of the divide. A jury watched videotaped footage of the severe beating of Rodney King and then, in essence, said that the police officers were within their rights to use such force. The first and most obvious response was the rage that was set loose by this verdict. Portions of Los Angeles went up in flames, and widespread looting occurred. An

African American friend of mine who is very committed to the principles of nonviolence reported having the desire to go out on the street and punch the first police officer he saw. This sense of outrage was not experienced by many whites. The prevailing attitude seemed to be that even if the verdict was wrong, so was the subsequent rage. While many whites disagreed with the verdict, some believed that the police officers were just a few "bad apples" in an otherwise good system of law enforcement. Persons of color often saw these police officers as the tip of an iceberg in a corrupt system. Interestingly, the media portrayed the "riot" or "rebellion" as a black event. Yet a majority of those arrested for looting were Hispanic, and whites accounted for 10 percent of the arrests.[1] Many of the businesses burned or looted were owned by Koreans and Latinos. I heard someone call this the first multicultural riot in the history of the United States.

The events surrounding the verdicts in the Rodney King case gathered much attention, and a flurry of books appeared that discussed the state of race relations in the United States. One was even provocatively titled *The Coming Race Wars?*[2] Yet the core issues undergirding our distrust and division remained largely unaddressed and unchanged. The nation went back to business as usual. Unfortunately, the seeds for a growing sense of isolation had been planted. So in 1995 when the second notable Los Angeles courtroom "not guilty" verdict was announced, America reawakened to the fact of the great divide in our country. The intensity of the diverse responses to the verdict shocked many. For others it confirmed the belief that all is not well in this nation that declares "liberty and justice for all."

The reactions to the verdict in the O. J. Simpson trial brought to the surface the multiplicity of divisions in society. Certainly the racial gulf was clearly seen. The reactions of many African Americans and whites differed dramatically. When the verdicts were announced, many African Americans cheered and applauded. This was interpreted by some whites as a case of African Americans celebrating the release of "one of their own." Yet many of those who were cheering stated that their joy was rooted in finally seeing the system work for a black man. (They believed that there was clearly reasonable doubt of Simpson's guilt.) Some whites questioned whether the predominantly African American jury was biased, too emotional, or lacking in intellectual astuteness. The fact that the white jurors also voted for acquittal seemed irrelevant. Some whites decided that the judicial system was broken. Some people of color responded that they had known this for years.

In the weeks following the acquittal, the race issue took some new turns. Questions began to surface concerning O. J. Simpson's behavior. Had Simpson assimilated into wealthy white society, turned to African Americans in his time of need, and then returned to his life of elitism after the trial ended? Also white racist backlash, previously held down by a semblance of civility, began to rear its ugly head. Some whites began to speak of the need to isolate themselves completely from African Americans. Some thought that African Americans should be cut off from any kind of government funding, while a few said that blacks should be given any financial help they needed in an effort to appease them.

Many women were visibly grieved at the announcement of the verdict. Their intense responses to the verdict, though disregarded by many, highlighted the deep divide in our society along gender lines. Whether or not women believed there was reasonable doubt that Simpson had committed murder, the evidence seemed very convincing that he had physically and emotionally abused his ex-wife, Nicole Brown-Simpson. Those grieving the verdict were expressing the concern that women who were being abused would be afraid to press charges against the batterer or even call for help because a high-profile abuser had gotten off. This did prove true: the number of calls to domestic-abuse hot lines decreased greatly during the days following the announcement of the verdict.

The trial of O. J. Simpson thrust class issues into the discussion as well. Some citizens felt that he had used his wealth to "buy" justice. Others responded that the only way a black man could receive a fair trial in America was to have a lot of money. If this had not been the trial of a rich black man, they felt, the jurors would never have found "reasonable doubt," and Simpson would have been sentenced to death row in a very short trial. Division along the lines of ethnicity and religion also emerged. The head lawyer, Johnnie Cochran, compared police officer Mark Fuhrman to Adolf Hitler and the actions of the Los Angeles police department to the events of the Holocaust. Robert Shapiro, a Jewish lawyer on the team, announced after the trial how offended he had been by these comparisons. Some objected to Johnnie Cochran's use of bodyguards from the Nation of Islam. They wondered what statement he was trying to make by building a relationship with the Nation of Islam while at the same time wearing a cross around his neck.

The response to these two courtroom verdicts illustrates the extent of our separation from each other. Many barriers limit our attempts to make reconciliation a reality. Some of these roadblocks to unity are the result of historic choices made by our society. Choices such as the enslavement of Africans on American soil, the genocide of Native Americans, the disenfranchisement of women, and the exploitation of immigrants, refugees, the poor, and others continue to impede our present endeavors at relational bridge building. Additional barriers are erected by individual choices: our decisions about where we live and with whom we socialize, but also our belief in stereotypes, our refusal to change, our infliction of abuse on others, our self-absorption, our denial of the problem, and so on.

Even the church impedes the reconciliation it preaches. We who claim to be followers of Jesus Christ find ourselves struggling with the reality that the same walls we construct in society are found in our Christian community. We allow the fact that we are created female and male to keep us apart. We embrace class distinctions. We segregate ourselves by racial designations. We exalt theological differences at the price of unity. We use cultural diversity as an excuse for division. This divide in the community of Jesus Christ creates perceptions that further perpetuate our separation. Because we in the human family do not seem to understand one another, our perspectives on life are frequently at odds. In this and the following chapter, I examine some of the obstacles that limit, undermine, and sabotage attempts at reconciliation. Because most of the forces of division outside Christianity are, unfortunately, also evident in the church, I illustrate our separation in both contexts.

As we examine barriers in our society, we will focus on what creates and perpetuates "dividing boundaries."[3] Some are imposed by society to designate differences (such as racial caste), but even the boundaries used by groups for self-identification (such as cultural heritage) also can become dividing boundaries when they presuppose group superiority. One could write an entire book on barriers—what the apostle Paul called "the dividing wall . . . the hostility between us" (Ephesians 2:14)—and many have. Because we are focusing here on the process of reconciliation, we do need to understand what we are up against. Given the scope of the book, the discussion is necessarily brief, and the list of barriers discussed is certainly not exhaustive. I am providing snapshots of the problem, glimpses of our estrangement that will root our discussion of unity in the reality of our challenge. In chapter 1, I investigate the barriers of isolation, injustice, exhaustion, betrayal, and denial. In chapter 2, I look closely at assimilation, tokenism, inferiority, rage, and fear. Then in chapter 3, I consider the possibility that Christian faith itself has become a barrier.

Isolation

I remember attending a meeting for African American ministers from a predominantly white denomination. The invited speaker was a white denominational official. As he spoke, he expressed his desire to learn how to worship like "your people" do. He continued in his attempt to connect with the assembled group of African American ministers by stating that "you people" could "teach me a lot." What had begun as a gathering of ministers united in their commitment to Christ turned into a meeting that created a feeling of separation between the speaker and "you people." It is easy to perceive life this way: me and everybody else. Any group can classify others as "you people" or "those people." Isolation is not merely an issue of geography; it is rooted in one's perception of life. Next-door neighbors may not have a clue about each other's understanding of life. This is true in the place of work and in the house of worship.

Our different ways of experiencing, and therefore interpreting, life can be based on gender, race, culture, economics, nationality, age, physical or mental abilities, sexual orientation, appearance, and a host of other factors. When our perceptions do not intersect with those of others through dialogue and shared experiences, we are isolated. When we experience life from an isolated perspective, we have no real knowledge of others. A lack of dialogue and honest sharing with others can result in a de facto segregation.

Often isolation is based on a simple lack of information about the lives of others, and this ignorance, if left unaddressed, can reinforce stereotypes and insensitivity. Although ignorance can be corrected by education, it is sometimes intentional: some folks do not want to know. But ignorance is not bliss! And clothing it in the language of preference does not make it more acceptable. This kind of ignorance may be seen in such comments as "We don't want that gospel music here" or "Why do those women always insist on inclusive language?" As biblical scholar and noted preacher James Earl Massey has observed, when a preference becomes "so important that deep emotion is stirred when it is not honored or satisfied, then that preference has become as forceful as an active prejudice—*perhaps it really cloaks a prejudice.*"[4] Ignorance, especially when it is rooted in a self-centered preference, isolates.

Isolation is a major roadblock to reconciliation. Our commitment to unlocking relational gridlock may be questioned if it is expressed at a distance (geographically or experientially). Women and people of color may wonder about the intentions of white males who invite them to the table in the workplace but exclude them from decision making in social settings. Urban folks may question the commitment of suburbanites who drive in to work on projects in poor neighborhoods and then return home before the sun sets.

At times, some who feel oppressed choose separation as a method of survival. Individuals desire to spend time with their "own" group as a means of cultural preservation. It may be necessary at times to gather for support, particularly when shared experiences in society are hostile or demeaning. Such gathering should be supported and in fact may be a necessary prelude to reconciliation. Yet it must be done within the broader context of membership in the human family; otherwise it isolates us. Isolation, whether based in ignorance or personal choice, whether imposed for good or bad reasons, ultimately limits the possibility for reconciliation.

Injustice

Injustice remains one of the strongest impediments to our coming together and certainly plays a major role in creating the isolation that must be overcome. Systemic injustice is at the root of many inequities in our society: where we can live and work, who makes the decisions that affect our lives, how we perform educationally and economically, and what we dare hope for in life. Our gender, our race, our economic status, our sexual orientation, our cultural background, our accent—all have an impact on our opportunity for success or failure. For some, this scenario serves as an advantage. For others, it complicates, to varying degrees, future hopes and dreams. Our respective positions on an uneven playing field greatly influence our view of the need for reconciliation. Those in the position of advantage may feel no need to create a just society. Those who feel disadvantaged may see attempts at reconciliation as a means to an end rather than a real path to unity.

This barrier to unity remains so formidable because, without any awareness, we seem to inherit the attitudes that help keep injustice in place. It is as though bigotry is a part of the air we breathe. Prejudice is in the culture, and we seem to acquire it without knowing it. As long as society creates new bigots, lasting reconciliation will be undermined. Sociologist C. Eric Lincoln calls race a "cultural fiction,"

> an emotional crutch for people whose sense of personal adequacy is threatened. It is the joker in a deck stacked for personal advantage in a game of life where the dealer must always win to break even. But in the world of objective reality, the alleged pure and definable race does not exist. . . . If race does not exist in reality, it exists with the *force* of reality and the *consequences* of reality in the minds of enough Americans to seriously qualify most orders of relationships between groups and among individuals.[5]

I think we could also say that bias based on gender is a biological fiction. Although biological differences between the sexes do not support belief in a superior or inferior rank within society, this belief has become a reality in the minds of enough people to affect relationships and institutions as well as images in popular culture. Class could be thought of as a status fiction. God does not declare one person more valuable than another because of wealth, celebrity status, power, or prestige. Yet because enough people have accepted such markers as a governing reality in our world, class distinctions order our understanding of relationships.

We continue to breed new bigots because our culture is infected with injustice. The blessing or curse of one's birth is accentuated by the systems that keep groups in or out of power from generation to generation. London professor Elaine Storkey describes the impact of systemic injustice on women when she writes that "pay differentials, educational priorities, rape, domestic violence, pornography, workloads in the home, leisure patterns all produce their own experience to indicate the extent of the problem. For it is woven into the very structure of contemporary society." Storkey further reminds us that advantages for males are built into the system: "Big careers for men are massaged by multinational corporations, professional bodies, employment agencies and the Civil Service. The links of the establishment pass through schools, clubs and associations which are exclusively male."[6] Without access to organizations and relationships that provide passage into future opportunities, women's choices, as well as those for people of color and people who are poor, are greatly reduced.

Sexism, classism, racism, and other forms of discrimination have also penetrated the church and taken up residence in Christian organizations. Some attribute the inability of women and people of color to move into positions of leadership in numbers that reflect their percentage of the total population to the existence of a "stained glass ceiling." This stained glass ceiling that systematically keeps certain people from participating fully in the life of the church seems contrary to the apostle Paul's great statement summarizing the impact of Christian faith: "There is no longer Jew or Greek, there is no longer slave or free, there is no longer male or female; for all of you are one in Christ Jesus" (Galatians 3:28). For many, this statement is an ideal that is rarely made real. If we are honest, we must admit that because of the stained glass ceiling, in the church it is a great advantage to be male, white, and economically secure. Systems of injustice in society and in the church exact a heavy cost on those outside the centers of power and effectively block reconciliation.

Exhaustion

Given the staying power of structural injustice, exhaustion becomes a major reason that people give up on reconciliation. Racial reconciler Spencer Perkins calls this "race fatigue."[7] We could also speak of gender fatigue, class fatigue, bigotry fatigue, and poverty fatigue. People who daily press against the walls of systemic injustice while simultaneously dealing with the individual bigots that they encounter have little energy left for efforts toward unity. People who are privileged yet choose to struggle against injustice also experience this exhaustion. Sometimes we can find ourselves feeling *too tired to care* about a oneness that seems so improbable.

I have met a number of people who have worked hard for reconciliation but have just burned themselves out physically, emotionally, and spiritually. I have seen this happen, for example, to persons of color who participate in the life of predominantly white Christian organizations. It may also happen to women struggling for gender equality and to whites working for social justice. The following cycle of experience comes from my observations of and conversations with several persons of color at a number of locations over a period of years. (I sincerely hope that this cycle is not representative of all predominantly white Christian organizations.) When the individual first arrives, he or she is excited about being at a Christian institution. The honeymoon experience fades when the person encounters the prejudice of an individual or encounters some subtle bias in the organizational system. These incidents are often hard to prove, and the person may be told that he or she is being "too sensitive." The next phase is one of activism. The person attempts to change the institution and make it more perceptive and just—in other words, more Christian. When little change takes place, the individual becomes depressed and despondent. Finally, he or she begins to look for a way to leave. (For the Christian college student, this cycle often correlates with the four years in a bachelor's program. It becomes almost unbearable if a student must come back for a fifth year.) A few times through this cycle would leave anyone short of energy, without hope for reconciliation, and just too tired to care.

Betrayal

Some people give up on building bridges of unity or feel too tired to care because they were betrayed when individuals or groups offered words of commitment with no follow-through. Reconciliation is held suspect when people see a history of broken promises. Like the popular phrase "Been there, done that, bought the T-shirt," broken promises are a familiar theme for far too many people. I heard some folks respond to news about the Promise Keepers movement by asking how its organizers were addressing the promise breakers. Unfortunately, people of color, people who are poor, and women meet all too often with promise breakers. The history of the United States is full of broken promises. For many, the American dream, the Emancipation Proclamation, women's rights, and treaties with Native Americans are examples of unfulfilled commitments and unrealized hopes.

According to theologian James Newton Poling, a cycle of debate and betrayal keeps evil systems of oppression in place and virtually undisturbed while serving the interests of the elite. He contends that, during certain periods in history, reconciliation and social justice seem within reach. The cycle begins when voices of hope bring their demands for social change to the broader public. I am reminded of the effect of Martin Luther King Jr.'s "I Have a Dream" speech at the March on Washington in 1963. Many people believed that racial unity was just a few years away. Poling suggests that once real change seems possible, this hopeful debate is re-pressed and systems of injustice are re-entrenched. From the vantage point of the 1990s, King's dream did not arrive for most people and in many cases was replaced by a nightmare.[8] Poling notes that in this cycle of debate and betrayal, "Public debate not only creates opportunities for new moral claims to be asserted, but also enables those who have power to reconceive their interests in more effective ways. During times of transition, debate, which offers oppressed groups the hope of social change, in fact betrays their trust, as those with power close ranks against the groups they had prom-ised to support."[9] People who feel betrayed in their attempt to redeem the promises of society may become bitter and angry. Broken promises create a sense of betrayal that makes rhetoric about reconciliation seem empty and meaningless.

Denial

An article in *Honolulu* magazine stated that one of the most prevalent myths in the island paradise is that "there's no racism in Hawai'i."[10] Like betrayal, denial is a serious road-block to any realistic attempt to create harmony. Denial is evident when our reply to the suggestion of prejudice is "I am not a ___ ist! There is no ___ ism here!" Even when confronted with evidence in the form of statistics or anecdo-tal data, we are tempted to respond, "It is not that bad!" We find it easier to deny reality than to deal with it.[11] The late Howard Thurman, a theologian and insightful commentator on issues of race, described the response of many whites living in a segregated society: "There is a natural resistance in being disturbed by having the moral question raised about segregation. But always there is a sneaking rumor that will not be silenced: all is not well behind the walls. It may be the chance acquaintance with [an African American] who pulls aside the curtain of the countenance and recalls a true view of the inner landscape." Thurman suggested that "often such awakening catapults one on the defensive. The most common remark is that the true picture is not understood."[12]

We may find ourselves in denial because we have been awakened or disturbed by the moral observation that all is not well behind the walls. Some of us are simply afraid to take a look at our own bigotry (inherited or otherwise). Such self-analysis is too painful. Others want to hide in the fantasy land of their own comfortable way of life and are offended by any interruption from an "ugly" reality. As incredible as it may seem, some folks are convinced that if they deny the reality of racism, classism, sexism, or other forms of bigotry, it does not exist—at least not for them. Therefore, in their minds, there is no need to discuss, or even think about, reconciliation.

Isolation, injustice, exhaustion, betrayal, and denial are costly problems. These dividing walls negatively influence our ways of thinking and perceiving. They affect our ability and willingness to engage in efforts that might lead to reconciliation. They seriously influence our daily reality, as well as the hopes and dreams we have for the future. The price of separation affects individual lives, societal harmony, and spiritual vibrancy. In the next chapter I continue this exploration by examining some barriers that either are created by hostility or are a response to it.

Questions for Discussion

1. Of the barriers described in chapter 1, which have you experienced or observed?

2. Describe the feeling of isolation. How do you think being isolated might affect someone? Identify as many ways as possible that people find themselves isolated in society.

3. Define *injustice*. Do you feel injustice is a problem in your community? Give some concrete examples of how you see it operating. Is there a "stained glass ceiling" in your church?

4. Identify times that you have experienced a sense of exhaustion because of the obstacles you faced in life. How did you find rest or gain a renewed sense of energy? Have you ever experienced fatigue because of racism, sexism, classism, or other forms of bigotry? If so, describe what made it an exhausting experience.

5. Have you ever been betrayed? How did it affect you? Cite some examples of broken promises in society and how they affect those expecting to benefit from the promises.

6. Why do people deny the existence of bigotry? Describe some ways that denial functions in society and in the church with regard to the racism, sexism, and classism of both individuals and institutions.

7. From reading this chapter, what is the most important insight you gained regarding division?

2

The Hostility between Us

While on a trip in Europe, James Earl Massey found himself at a train station in Basel, Switzerland, waiting to depart to his next destination. His thoughts were interrupted by the sound of a woman asking, in American English, on which platform she could find the train to Zurich. Massey looked up from the book he was reading to observe the situation that was developing. The person to whom the woman had addressed her question responded, "Bitte, nicht verstehen Sie!"—"I am not understanding you." The American woman then directed her question to the next person and received the same reply. By the time she received the same response in German a third time, she had moved very close to where Massey was waiting. Yet after the third attempt she shouted, "What dummies! Does nobody here speak English?"

Massey relates his feelings at that moment: "Her arrogance made me freeze. I had wanted to help her but her tribal notion of being a privileged American made me hesitate as a partial rebuke of her spirit. Crediting ignorance to the Swiss travelers around me, and invisibility to me, a black, the white woman marched out of the area still fuming in an arrogant anxiety." Massey adds: "If she had only turned in my direction! If only her eyes had not been blinded by the racist notion of a white American hierarchical order, she might have seen me, ventured the question, 'Do you speak English?'—and received instant help from me. But no. Her arrogance blocked me and limited her. Arrogance always limits us."[1]

The woman who ignored James Earl Massey and insulted the Swiss travelers was practicing "plantation protocol."[2] She presumed that it was her right by birth to treat others in an arrogant, condescending, and patronizing manner. Many people of color, women, low-income individuals, and persons with a "foreign" accent can witness to similar experiences. I believe that such an attitude of superiority is a direct challenge to the position of God in this world and a form of self-idolatry. In truth, only God is superior. The rest of us are neither inferior nor superior. We are all equally created in the image of God. Yet this kind of arrogance seems to possess many individuals and permeate many of our institutions. It has created a "hostility between us" in our society (Ephesians 2:14). As long as this "plantation protocol" remains unacknowledged, unchallenged, and unchanged, true reconciliation is blocked from even being considered. In this chapter I examine what I believe are two pillars supporting this false sense of superiority: assimilation and tokenism. Then I explore three intense feelings produced by the hostility that is elicited by attempts to impose superiority: inferiority, rage, and fear.

Assimilation

Some of the arrogance manifested by individuals like the woman whom James Earl Massey encountered is created by attempts at assimilation. According to the notion of the melting pot in the United States, individuals from all racial and cultural groups are melted into one new race—the American race. On the surface this notion seems harmless and almost noble. In some ways it actually sounds like the Christian ideal of finding a common identity in Christ. Persons were to find their common identity in being "American." One was to come to the United States and let go of her or his culture and language (if it was not English) and become American, which primarily meant adopting the culture of a white Anglo-Saxon Protestant.[3] One clear example of this pressure can be seen in the boarding schools created for Native American children. The children were taken away from their parents and put through a process that involved "giving the child a new and 'proper name,' a uniform, cutting short the long hair of the boys, and communicating to these children in numerous other ways that the Indian way was bad and the white way was good."[4] Even the term *America* is often meant to be synonymous with the United States rather than inclusive of Canada, Mexico, and countries in Central and South America.

The assumption that everyone wants to put on white Anglo-Saxon cultural attire has created tremendous pressure to assimilate, with dire effects on both people of color and whites. Theologian Fumitaka Matsuoka describes this process: "Historically when a dominant group has wished to subjugate a certain group of people in this society in the name of unity, it has first made them subhuman." He continues: "In such a societal setting, the 'unity' means the protection of the dominant group and its culture rather than a representational and mutual sharing of 'life-together.'"[5] Assimilation often means a loss of cultural self-understanding for all involved. Some people of color may be tempted to try to "out-white" the whites. Matsuoka observes that people of color can find themselves "in an untenable position between the ever-present reminder of [a] 'racial uniform,' which isolates [them] from full participation in society, and equally powerful forces toward acculturation into the dominant European American culture."[6]

While it has been devastating for people of color to reject their culture of origin in an attempt to become American, even white Europeans who move to the United States can face the same pressures to let go of their "foreigner" status and become "white Americans." Some years ago a distinguished lecturer from a European country was touring the United States at a time when his country was not highly esteemed by everyone. His first lecture was given at a place where people admired him, and he included a story to build rapport with the audience. "The upstairs maid in a certain home answered the telephone: 'Yes—yes—it certainly is,' and hung up. She then said to the lady of the house, 'Some lady on the phone wanted to know if this was the residence of Mrs. Smith. When I said yes, then she wanted to know if Mrs. Smith was at home, and I said yes. Then she made a funny remark, 'It's a long distance from New York,' and I answered, 'It certainly is,' and hung up."

At the next location where he was to give the same lecture, the people were more critical of the appropriateness of his speaking in their town. At the point in his lecture where the story came, he made some slight changes. Rather than saying "yes," he said "yes, ma'am." He also changed "it certainly is" to "it shure is," trying to mock a so-called black dialect. At the third place where he was to lecture, the mood was angry and many had protested his appearance. This time he told the story again with the so-called black dialect but also identified the person as a "Negro maid." The "foreigner" felt the need to make sure that his audience understood that he was as white as they were. He did this by demonstrating that he shared their prejudices and arrogance in an attempt to "out-white" his perception of what it meant to be white.[7]

Assimilation in the United States has ramifications beyond the racial and cultural realms. Some women are told that they have to act like a man if they want to succeed in a "man's world." For poor people, assimilation may mean that they are supposed to want what rich folks have. People from non-Christian religions often are expected to conform to the calendar of Christian holidays and to celebrate their own sacred traditions unobtrusively. This emphasis on uniformity impedes reconciliation. Many Christians try to avoid issues of diversity, whether of race, culture, gender, or class, by asking, "Can't we all be one in Christ?" This often really means "Can't we all be like me or my group?"

In reality, assimilation does not work. I was born left-handed in a right-handed world. My grandmother, who was born left-handed, was forced to be right-handed. Because society was designed for righties, she was forced to assimilate. Some people who write left-handed have tried to "act right-handed" by writing upside down in a contorted fashion, simulating a right-handed style. I learned to play sports right-handed, but I have often wondered if I would do better as a lefty. Did I lose something by not following my natural orientation? Although we are told that there is equal opportunity for left-handers in this right-handed world, many schoolrooms do not even have desks for lefties. Forced assimilation would be a joke if it were not so painful. Reconciliation is not having everybody do everything the same way. Assimilation is cheap reconciliation. It blocks genuine efforts at coming together.

Tokenism

The concept of assimilation has been adapted through the years to allow people who do not fit the preestablished mold to retain some of their cultural identity. One can retain some of one's difference as long as it does not get in the way of the dominant culture. One must know how to "act white" or "act like a man" or "act middle class" if the occasion requires it. In fact, persons from the dominant group must be so comfortable around you that they can remark that "you are not like the others." For people of color such an exception means a designation of honorary Caucasian status. A woman who tones down her assertiveness, ignores sexist behavior, and avoids rocking the boat may at times qualify as an honorary man. When the dominant group needs an opinion, this individual becomes the token representative, expected to speak for everyone of his or her race or gender who lives (or has lived) in this world.

Malcolm X likened this experience of being the token to being the "house Negro." During slavery, he observed,

> There were two kinds of Negroes. There was that old house Negro and the field Negro. And the house Negro always looked out for his master. When the field Negroes got too much out of line, he held them back in check. He put 'em back on the plantation.
>
> The house Negro could afford to do that because he lived better than the field Negro. He ate better, he dressed better, and he lived in a better house. He lived right up next to his master—in the attic or the basement. He ate the same food his master ate and wore his same clothes. And he could talk just like his master—good diction. And he loved his master more than his master loved himself. That's why he didn't want his master hurt.
>
> If the master got sick, he'd say, "What's the matter, boss, *we* sick?" When the master's house caught afire, he'd try and put the fire out. He didn't want his master's house burned. He never wanted his master's property threatened. And he was more defensive of it than the master was. That was the house Negro.
>
> But then you had some field Negroes, who lived in huts, had nothing to lose. They wore the worst kind of clothes. They ate the worst food. And they caught hell. They felt the sting of the lash. They hated their master. Oh yes, they did.
>
> If the master got sick, they'd pray that the master died. If the master's house caught fire, they'd pray for a strong wind to come along. This was the difference between the two.
>
> And today you still have house Negroes and field Negroes. I'm a field Negro. If I can't live in the house as

a human being, I'm praying for a wind to come along. If the master won't treat me right and he's sick, I'll tell the doctor to go in the other direction. But if all of us are going to live as human beings, as brothers, then I'm for a society of human beings that can practice brotherhood.[8]

This master-slave paradigm, as exemplified in the house Negro syndrome, is still played out in some corporations and organizations, including those that wear the tag of Christian. Such organizations will seek to hire persons of color or women who they believe will be inoffensive and harmless. These individuals are expected to be the experts on all issues related to their gender or race. They may be called on to instruct, console, or quiet others who look like themselves. They are expected to endorse the company line. While they are often paid well, the loss of their job is always a possibility; advancement is based on loyalty, and they are expected to embrace the "we are all one" theory of assimilation.

Hospital chaplain Al Miles describes a situation he faced while serving as the director of pastoral care at a hospital. He was summoned by the president of the hospital to help resolve a heated dispute involving a patient. It soon became apparent that Miles, an African American, had been called in on the situation only because the patient was also an African American. It also became clear that the president was expecting him to confirm that racism did not occur at the hospital. Miles felt that he was being asked to be "the Black Prince who could save [the] hospital from a lawsuit."[9] He reflects: "Racism not only involves putting an individual or group in an inferior position, but it also deals with setting them apart in other ways. It is offensive because it robs people of their dignity, power, and respect, reducing them to nothing more than an object." Miles continues, "I was the 'House Nigger.' I had drunk the fine wine and eaten from the fatted calf reserved primarily for the Master and his family. I acted, dressed and spoke just like them. So I was expected to stand by them."[10]

Al Miles refused to play the role expected of him and even told the hospital's president that he not only had observed racism at the hospital but had personally experienced it several times (he no longer works at that hospital). Unlike Miles in that situation, some women and people of color may choose to remain silent and support the party line because they feel they cannot afford to lose their job and impose financial hardship on their family. Tokenism has a devastating effect on the relationship between the person being tokenized and the tokenizer. The token is not really seen as a person but simply represents the perception of women or people of color held by the person in power. So while the individual cast in the role of a token may choose to hide her or his real individuality and feelings, the person in the position of power is developing a relationship with a figment of his or her imagination. Obviously, reconciliation cannot be accomplished in such an environment.

Inferiority

One of the primary effects of constantly feeling that you are a token can be a powerful sense of inferiority. A person may have tried to assimilate but is still considered inferior to the dominant group because of her race, culture, gender, or class. He may feel like an illegitimate American or possibly an illegitimate Christian. After hearing words like (or being treated as) the weaker sex, white trash, disadvantaged, minority, other, incapable, or even worse, one may, on some level, begin to believe what is being said or implied. Christian community development activist Spencer Perkins describes the insidious nature of the residual self-doubt and the pervasive sense of inferiority that can torment one's mind: "You must remember, you're black. You don't come from as stable a background as these white people. No black person has ever held this position before. If you don't succeed in this task, you will let down the whole black race." Such thoughts play like a melancholy refrain damaging one's self-esteem. One can be haunted by the question posed by Perkins: "Don't the years of oppression of my people make me less capable— don't they make me, in fact, inferior?"[11]

Given the constant barrage of comments and innuendos regarding one's supposed inferiority, an individual may develop a strong need to be found worthy. Some people who experience the effects of inferiority believe the messages they are receiving and blame themselves and others who have been victimized. This internalization of a victim's mind-set presumes that people in power have an inborn right to exert control over others, so persons *not* holding the strings of power in a relationship may feel that they have to prove themselves worthy of being included. A person of color may experience the desire to prove herself or himself to be as good as a white person. A woman may feel that she must demonstrate that she is as competent as a man. The poor person may be tempted to put on a facade of economic privilege. A person who believes that he or she is inferior may not feel worthy of being reconciled to others.

Rage

A lifetime of pain fueled by injustice, betrayal, denial, condescension, tokenism, and feelings of inferiority produces emotional distress and deep scars in the psyche and the spirit. This feeling of worthlessness and personal pain can lead to anger and rage. Legitimate anger provides evidence of the magnitude of our suffering and the extent to which our emotional, psychological, and spiritual health is in peril. Afro-American studies professor Catherine Meeks gives expression to the feelings of rage that may be evident for some in the context of race relations in the United States:

> We hate you because we have not begun to forgive you or your ancestors for their enslavement of our ancestors; nor

have we forgiven you for today's oppression of us, which comes primarily from the system that you protect and rule. . . .

As long as we talk about reconciliation without acknowledging our very real and legitimate rage, we are trying to have a manipulated reconciliation. . . . It is not enough to say that you didn't have anything to do with slavery and that you don't feel guilty about it. Perhaps you don't have a sense of guilt, but blacks and whites share a collective history, and just as blacks have to deal with slavery, so do whites.

As a white person you are a partner in the oppression which your foreparents created. The denial of this partnership has created a lot of pseudo-relating between whites and blacks. This type of pseudo-relating comes across as patronizing liberalism, and the world is not in need of more patronizing liberals. The denial of the feelings around this issue on the part of whites simply adds fuel to the fires of mistrust and deepens the wounds of both races.[12]

Our society is consumed by anger about sexism, fewer job opportunities, racism, "reverse discrimination," classism, shrinking incomes, crime, anti-Semitism, stereotypes, religious pluralism, and on and on. In the midst of such outrage, reconciliation can get lost or misused in the debate.

Fear

In addition to rage, there is also more than enough fear to go around. Science fiction writer Ray Bradbury captured the fears of whites regarding their relationship with African Americans when he wrote the short story "The Other Foot" in 1951.[13] The story's premise is that African Americans left planet Earth because of racism and colonized Mars. Twenty years later a spaceship from Earth is headed toward Mars. This will be the first contact between the races since African Americans left Earth. (Earth had destroyed all its rockets in a nuclear war and only now had been able to rebuild one.) Many African Americans on Mars organize to welcome the whites by giving them a taste of the experience of segregation. One character, Willie, describes it this way: "Well, the shoe's on the other foot now. We'll see who gets laws passed against him, who gets lynched, who rides the back of streetcars, who gets segregated in shows." He continues his impromptu speech: "They can come up and live and work here; why, certainly. All they got to do to deserve it is live in their own small part of town, the slums, and shine our shoes for us, and mop up our trash, and sit in the last row in the balcony. That's all we ask. And once a week we hang one or two of them. Simple."[14]

When the white man from Earth finally arrives, he emerges from the spaceship and describes the fate that has befallen Earth. After the African Americans had left Earth, World War III erupted. Nearly every city was destroyed, and Earth is completely radioactive. Only a small number of people remain on Earth, and they are requesting the chance to come to Mars and start over. The white man pleads: "We'll come and work [the soil] for you. Yes, we'll even do that. We deserve anything you want to do to us, but don't shut us out." He adds with urgency: "We'll come here and we'll work for you and do the things you did for us—clean your houses, cook your meals, shine your shoes, and humble ourselves in the sight of God for the things we have done over the centuries to ourselves, to others, to you."[15]

The white man's plea caught the attention of some. Once it became clear that all the places, signs, and perpetrators of past injustices had been completely destroyed, the mood shifted. Willie summed up the feelings of the group: "The time for being fools is over. We got to be something else except fools. I knew that when he talked. I knew then that now the white man's as lonely as we've always been. He's got no home now, just like we didn't have one for so long.

Now everything's even. We can start all over again, on the same level." He added pensively, "Seems like for the first time today I really seen the white man—I really seen him clear."[16]

This story speaks of the fear of retribution that some of us carry way down deep in our souls. Maybe we have never intentionally been a racist, or a classist, or a sexist, but others have, and we fear that we will pay for their crimes. The story also holds out the hope for forgiveness from the offended and their descendants for past and present sins. Interestingly, while Bradbury's story reminds us of our fears, it invests its hope in the belief that the oppressed are more moral than the oppressors and will be forgiving. It was up to African Americans in the story to recognize the humanity of whites, for whites knew of the brutality against African Americans by people of their race and questioned their own humanity until it was validated by African Americans.

Some do not accept Bradbury's hopes for reconciliation. One of Thomas Jefferson's greatest fears was that a slave revolt could turn into a race war. (The idea of a race war still lingers.) He lamented, "If something is not done, and soon done, we shall be the murderers of our children."[17] A larger police force, more prisons, repression of human rights, and other methods of control are sometimes recommended for addressing fears of retribution. Howard Thurman noted the intensity of the fear of retribution among whites in the United States during the era of legalized segregation:

> A white society must array all the forces of legislation and law enforcement: it must falsify the facts of history, tamper with the insights of religion and religious doctrine, editorialize and slant news and the printed word. On top of that it must keep separate schools, separate churches, separate graveyards, and separate public accommodations—all this in order to freeze the place of the [African American] in society and guarantee his

basic immobility. Yet all this is but partial indication of the high estimate that such a society places upon him. Once again, to state it categorically: The measure of a man's estimate of your strength is the kind of weapons he feels that he must use in order to hold you fast in a prescribed place. . . .

The form or the manifestation of this high regard or estimate is fear! It is not the fear of the strange and unfamiliar, but it is the fear of retribution and vengeance. There is a deep center of anxiety within white society that is created and sustained by an abiding sense of collective guilt, but held in place by the inverted notion of the strength and power of the [African American]. It is the ancient fear which the strong have of the weak.[18]

The fear of retribution is not the only fear that blocks reconciliation. There is the fear of the unknown and unexpected. We may fear that our efforts will be rejected or disapproved. Our fears may be rooted in a resistance to change our perceptions, our theology, or the way our world is ordered. It seems that our fears emerge out of our psyche with toxic intensity, choking and sabotaging our efforts at the very point when reconciliation becomes honest and real. The dividing walls of hostility described in this and the previous chapter are built upon societal norms and personal behavior. Some even represent cheap attempts at reconciliation. These roadblocks to unity are sober reminders of the cost of division and the challenge of reconciliation. In the next chapter we examine one additional barrier. It may be the most securely established obstacle, the most formidable threat to our hopes for reconciliation.

Questions for Discussion

1. Of the barriers described in chapter 2, which have you experienced or observed? List additional obstacles to unity that you are aware of. How do these limit reconciliation?

2. Do you agree with the author's contention that assimilation is cheap reconciliation? If not, why not? Suggest an alternative explanation. If so, why? Offer some current examples.

3. When you hear the word *token,* what images come to mind? Define *token.* Have you ever been treated as a token or observed a situation where someone else has been? How does such treatment affect a person? What needs to occur before tokenism can be eliminated?

4. Have you ever felt inferior? If so, identify how this made you feel. Give both some positive and negative examples of how people choose to respond to feelings of inferiority.

5. Have you ever experienced rage? Describe this feeling. Have you ever been on the receiving end of someone's rage? Can rage and reconciliation coexist? Explain.

6. Is the fear of retribution alive today? If so, how does it manifest itself? What are your fears regarding the divisions in society? Do you have any fears about the process of reconciliation? What are they?

7. What in this chapter helped you better understand why reconciliation seems so elusive in our world? Elaborate.

3

Which Jesus Is the Real Jesus?

Sojourner Truth was born a slave. At age nine she was sold and taken away from her parents. She gained her freedom at age thirty and named herself Sojourner Truth. She was a six-foot-tall preacher who worked for the freedom of both African American slaves and women. On one occasion she encountered some clergymen who were saying that if God had wanted women to be equal to men, God would have demonstrated this in the birth, life, and death of Jesus Christ. Sojourner Truth's response was: "He say women can't have as much rights as man, 'cause Christ warn't a woman. Whar did your Christ come from?" Then, speaking as loudly as she could, Sojourner Truth asked the question again, "Whar did your Christ come from?" After a brief pause she exclaimed: "From God and a woman! Man had nothing to do with him!"[1]

One Sunday evening a visitor from the west coast of Africa addressed a group of young people at an African American church. He remarked: "Since it was the Christian Sabbath, I decided to visit a church. The first church I found was on the other end of the street. When I entered I was told that I was at the wrong church. This was the First Baptist Church white and what I wanted was the First Baptist Church colored."

Then he exclaimed: "Allah laughs aloud in His Muslim
Heaven when He beholds the Christian spectacle: First Baptist Church colored! First Baptist Church white!"[2]

Some years ago I worked in the Times Square area of New
York City. As I walked the streets I was regularly approached
by people begging for money. I was concerned that the
money I gave would be used for drugs or alcohol, so I
sometimes informed folks that I could not give them any
money. This enabled me to feel confident that they were not
using money to harm themselves. I often thought to myself,
"I wish people would ask me to buy them something to eat.
That way I could be sure that they were using the money I
gave them appropriately." One day, while I was on my way
to a church service, a man approached me and asked if I
would buy him a sandwich. In my rush not to be late for the
worship service, I told the man that I did not have time to
help him.

The above episodes, representative of countless situations,
point to a spirit of hypocrisy at work within the life of the
church. Prejudice has taken up residence in many of us who
call ourselves Christians. Martin Luther King Jr.'s assessment
of the church in the 1960s rings true today. He stated: "It is
still true that the church is the most segregated major institution in America. As a minister of the gospel I am ashamed
to have to affirm that eleven o'clock on Sunday morning,
when we stand to sing, 'In Christ There Is No East Nor West,'
is the most segregated hour of America, and the Sunday
school is the most segregated school of the week."[3] It is easy
to observe that our congregations, denominations, and personal witness remain largely segregated by race, culture, and
class. Although not as visible to the outsider, in many congregations and church institutions sexism reigns unhindered. The church that emerged after Jesus Christ broke
down the walls of separation is now often the cornerstone of
a divided world. The early church's vision of unity is often

proclaimed with eloquent rhetoric but seldom expressed in reality. Not only is "Allah in His Muslim Heaven" laughing, but many others clearly see the divide between biblical proclamation and Christian action. Christians who are committed to addressing bigotry often find themselves, like Sojourner Truth, either embarrassed by or at odds with the institutional church. If we are honest with ourselves, we must admit that we sometimes fail to see Jesus in the person asking us for help (Matthew 25:31-46).

Society's Mirror

In this chapter I offer an "in-house" critique of Christianity as a barrier to reconciliation. The reason that Christianity often acts as a dividing wall rather than a uniting force is that instead of modeling the inclusiveness of Jesus Christ, it has mirrored the exclusiveness of society. Many of our churches reflect the broader society in the United States, which is divided by race, class, gender, culture, and ethnicity. Not only do churches reflect the separation found in society, but bigotry has been sustained by a portion of the institutional church from the very beginning of the history of the United States. The genocide of Native Americans was defended through the misapplication of Scripture texts about the conquest of the Canaanites. The enslavement of Africans was upheld by the church through the twisted use of the so-called curses of Cain and Ham (although Cain's family did not survive the flood and Ham was never cursed).[4] Anti-Semitism[5] was supported by the faulty notion that the Jews killed Jesus (although the Bible clearly states that Jesus met his death by Roman execution at the orders of a Roman governor named Pontius Pilate). Women were marginalized as the weaker gender and expected to submit unilaterally to men because of the sin of Eve (although Adam also sinned). The poor were revictimized by a "prosperity gospel" that found the evidence of God's blessing in material wealth (although Jesus said that the kingdom of God belonged to the poor).

The United States has never had to address seriously this contradiction in its stated commitment to freedom because its "conscience," the church, has compromised itself in the same way. When society looked at the church, it saw a mirror image of itself. Perhaps historian and former civil rights activist Calvin Morris sums it up best:

> Racist faith, that belief system which invests ultimate meaning in the biology of white skin color, has permeated American history from its beginning. . . . The founders of this nation faced a dilemma posed by the conflict between freedom and slavery. A people proclaiming as the bedrock of their political existence the concept of human liberty as a natural endowment given by God nonetheless held others in chains. Thus, the United States was founded upon political and moral ambiguities so profound that its characterization of itself as a land of freedom and human liberty has to it the sound of hypocrisy.[6]

A sexist faith that invests ultimate meaning in maleness and a classist faith that invests ultimate meaning in material wealth also demonstrate the hypocrisy of the United States and the church. In addition, the pervasive denominationalism of Christianity reflects nationalist tendencies, ideological influences, ethnic identities, class distinctions, racial rifts, and a host of other sociological forces. For many, Christianity is steeped in hypocrisy, and its inability to act as a reconciling force has been noted by occasional prophetic voices. A few examples follow:

> Our church, which has been fighting in these years only for its self-preservation, as though that were an end in itself, is incapable of taking the word of reconciliation and redemption to mankind and the world.[7]
>   —Dietrich Bonhoeffer

The result is that in the one place in which normal, free contacts might be most naturally established—in which relations of the individual to his God should take priority over conditions of class, race, power, status, wealth, or the like—this place is one of the chief instruments for guaranteeing barriers.[8]

—Howard Thurman

It is difficult to convey the message of reconciliation because most Christians are insensitive to the problem.[9]

—Samuel G. Hines

Exempt from the civil rights of the land, American churches have become a stronghold of resistance to the principles of justice and equality rather than the source of it.[10]

—Cheryl Sanders

Two Christian Faiths?

The struggle of Christianity to be a reconciling force in society is a source of real concern. Although the Bible speaks of the oneness of the human family and the ministry of reconciliation, the practice of many who call themselves Christians is hypocritical. Many so-called believers are living contradictions to the faith they proclaim. Psychologist Gordon Allport, in his classic study *The Nature of Prejudice*, notes this paradox: religion "makes prejudice and it unmakes prejudice. . . . Churchgoers are more prejudiced than the average; they are also less prejudiced than the average."[11] Allport further states that as a result of this dichotomy, people "judge religion not by its scriptural purity, but as it is perverted by a majority of its followers."[12] Thus the gospel of reconciliation can easily become ineffective. Though Allport's contention about the prejudices of religious believers may initially be hard to accept, simple observation of religious life and beliefs makes it tenable.

Significantly, a number of people have rejected Christianity

because of those who call themselves Christians. A number
of women have left the church because of its insensitivity to
the value and importance of inclusive language. People in
poverty may avoid church because of the showy materialism
of church members and the existence of unwritten "dress
codes." Mohandas Gandhi rejected Christianity when, because he was not white, he was refused entrance to a church
in South Africa where a minister friend of his was preaching.[13] The late E. Stanley Jones, missionary to India, said this
was racism's worst sin, "the obscuring of Christ in an hour
when one of the greatest souls born of woman was making
his decision."[14] Malcolm X, the son of a Baptist minister,
rejected Christianity because he observed that

> Christianity is the white man's religion. The Holy
> Bible in the white man's hands and his interpretations
> of it have been the greatest single ideological weapon
> for enslaving millions of non-white human beings.
> Every country the white man has conquered with his
> guns, he has always paved the way, and salved his
> conscience, by carrying the Bible and interpreting it
> to call the people "heathens" and "pagans"; then he
> sends his guns, and his missionaries behind the guns
> to mop up. . . .[15]

Gordon Allport informs us that religion can produce either
a faith that encourages prejudice and divisiveness or a faith that
nurtures reconciliation and inclusiveness. Allport summarizes
his discussion of religion and prejudice with these words:

> We have seen that [religion] may be of an ethnocentric
> order, aiding and abetting a life style marked by preju-
> dice and exclusiveness. Or it may be of a universalistic
> order, vitally distilling ideals of brotherhood into
> thought and conduct. Thus we cannot speak sensibly of
> the relation between religion and prejudice without
> specifying the sort of religion we mean and the role it
> plays in the personal life.[16]

So we are faced with the question: Which sort of Christianity are we practicing, and how does it affect our lifestyle and outlook? One could assume that there must be two, if not multiple, forms of Christianity existing side by side in the world. This reality is similar to what had begun to happen in the church at Corinth. Some were claiming to be followers of Paul's Christ, Peter's Christ, or Apollos's Christ, while others were claiming just to follow Christ (1 Corinthians 1:11-13). Perhaps this is the greatest challenge to reconciliation: the dividing wall erected by varied perceptions of Jesus, each of which has created its own faith understanding.

Which Jesus Is the Real Jesus?

Our modern understandings of Jesus are often a far cry from the real Jesus of Nazareth who walked the earth during the first century. We have misinterpreted, reinterpreted, misused, and remade Jesus to serve our own purposes. As we observe the modern-day representations of Jesus, we must ask, "Which Jesus is the real Jesus?"

the Jesus of the Democrats or the Jesus of the
    Republicans?
the Jesus of Billy Graham or the Jesus of Jesse Jackson?
the Jesus of Mother Teresa or the Jesus of Madonna?
the rich Jesus or the poor Jesus?
the Protestant Jesus or the Catholic Jesus?
the Baptist Jesus or the Methodist Jesus?
the black Jesus or the white Jesus?
the Asian Jesus or the Native American Jesus?
the high church Jesus or the holy roller Jesus?
the urban Jesus or the suburban Jesus?
Jesus Christ the superstar or Jesus Christ the suffering
    servant?
the Jesus portrayed in stained glass windows or the
    Jesus in the heart of blood-stained victims of
    violence?

Often, depending upon our life experiences, our respective understandings of Jesus are quite different. Women and men may perceive Jesus differently. Both the Re-Imagining Community[17] and the Promise Keepers movement claim to follow Jesus Christ. Is it the same Jesus? During slavery, both the slave master and the slave said they believed in Jesus Christ. Was it the same Jesus? Is the Jesus Christ who "blesses" some with wealth and the Jesus Christ who helps others survive in the midst of material poverty the same Jesus? Which Jesus is the real Jesus? This question confronts us with its urgency and gets to the heart of the issue: our lack of reconciliation. Yet this is not the first time such a question has been asked. It sounds hauntingly similar to the question that John the Baptist asked while in prison. He sent two of his disciples to Jesus with the question: "Are you the one who is to come, or are we to wait for another?" (Matthew 11:3; Luke 7:20). John's question has echoed through history. Many times all around the globe people have asked of the Jesus presented to them, "Are you the one who is to come, or are we to wait for another?"

Many people have asked John's question when presented with white images of Jesus.[18] The "brown Mary," Our Lady of Guadalupe, may have appeared in Mexico as the result of the Spanish missionaries' presentation of a royal white image of Jesus.[19] The people of Mexico did not recognize this as the real Jesus. Francisco Penning, a student of mine from Chile, shared his experience with me: "Once a week I would go with my aunt to the local church of the *barrio*. My aunt would kneel and pray to the Virgin Mary while I looked at all the statues of the saints and the cross of a beautiful, white, blond Jesus. Then I would see the tears in my aunt's eyes. I would keep looking around hoping that those statues somehow would hear my aunt's prayers." He reflects: "Today I ask myself why my aunt never prayed to that Jesus. Instead she prayed to a statue of a brown Virgin Mary that looks more like the people I know in South America. [Now I understand] that my aunt could relate to the Virgin, and I also understand why so many people in South America including myself never kneeled to the cross. My aunt's tears spoke of hard times, suffering, bread to put on the table for a family of 11. But who wants to hear the cries of a poor woman? That huge cross with Jesus in the center of the church was too much. His white, shiny skin portrayed a being foreign to those in the streets who I grew up with. The robe was of a red silk, the eyes were blue looking down at the empty seats. The white statue seemed indifferent to anybody coming with a humble prayer."[20]

Perhaps the question "Which Jesus is the real Jesus?" does not get asked because of what the answer will imply. I believe we do not ask the question in order to avoid the indictment of our sexism. As William Sloane Coffin, renowned social justice activist, states: "Christian men who still refuse to acknowledge their oneness and equality with women will continue not only to try to walk all over women at home, at work, and in the churches; climbing up on the cross to be seen from afar, they will also trample on the One who has hung there so long."[21] I believe that another reason this question rarely gets asked is summed up in noted preacher Mack King Carter's blunt response: "The greatest threat to America and its brand of Christianity was never Communism, but the fact that Jesus might have been a Black man." Carter continues: "If this could be proved photographically, Christianity would last only seventy-two hours: twenty-four hours to embrace the shock, twenty-four hours to pack its icons and religious paraphernalia, and twenty-four hours to deal with massive clerical unemployment. The dispersive power of ebony pigmentation is awesome! Just think of it, the Nigger from Nazareth is Lord!"[22]

Is our interpretation based only on our social location, or can we discover which Jesus is the real Jesus? Until this question is answered, our Christianity may be hypocritical, a roadblock to genuine reconciliation.[23] While much of modern Christianity appears to be a faith that divides, we must hold on to that faith in Jesus Christ that is inclusive. In the first three chapters I have painted a grim picture of the barriers to reconciliation. Chapter 4 provides hope. Here I present the biblical mandate to us to be ambassadors of reconciliation. I give particular attention to the example of Jesus and the impact of the early church in the ministry of reconciliation.

Questions for Discussion

1. Do you accept the premise that Christianity has been a barrier to reconciliation? If so, why? If not, why not?

2. Do you know anyone who has left the Christian faith (or the institutional church) because he or she felt that Christians were hypocrites? How did the person arrive at that conclusion? Do you have any ideas for correcting this problem?

3. In what ways does the contemporary church mirror society's values? Have you ever observed racist faith? sexist faith? or class-based faith? Describe what you saw.

4. What do you think of the notion that there are multiple forms of Christianity? If you accept this idea, list some examples.

5. How do you answer the question, Which Jesus is the real Jesus? Why did you answer the question as you did?

6. Is there room for different answers to the question, Which Jesus is the real Jesus? What would be the effect?

7. What in this chapter provoked your thinking in a new way? Why?

Part II

A Costly Proclamation

4

God's One-Item Agenda

Chris Rice, a member of the Voice of Calvary ministry in Mississippi, tells about a group of volunteers from the Midwest who spent a week with them in Jackson renovating a house for a low-income family. As part of the week-long experience, members of the Voice of Calvary staff prepared an authentic southern soul-food dinner for the group. Following the meal, during which several of the visiting volunteers complained about the food, Spencer Perkins, also of Voice of Calvary, shared a word about God's desire for racial reconciliation. This is at the heart of Voice of Calvary's reason for existence. When the message ended, an adult leader from the visiting Midwesterners said: "Thanks for the food, but I'm tired, and I came here to serve Christ, not to talk about black and white. So I'm going to leave." The other visitors left with him.[1]

This episode reveals a tragic misunderstanding of what it means to follow Jesus Christ. It also illustrates why the church not only has been ineffective in addressing societal fragmentation, but, as I illustrated in chapter 3, has contributed to it. "Serving Christ" cannot be divorced from "talking about black and white." That is like the apostle Paul saying he wanted to serve Christ rather than talk about healing the division between Jew and Gentile, male and female, slave and free. In fact, as we shall discover, this message of unity was at the very core of what the disciples understood as serving Jesus Christ. The late Samuel Hines, an urban pastor and a great expositor of reconciliation, made it very explicit: "God has a one-item agenda, listed in one expressive and inclusive word—Reconciliation."[2] Hines's audacious declaration was based on his study of the Bible, particularly Paul's eloquent articulation of the meaning of Jesus Christ's ministry in 2 Corinthians 5:17-20:

> So if anyone is in Christ, there is a new creation: everything old has passed away; see, everything has become new! All this is from God, who reconciled us to himself through Christ, and has given us the ministry of reconciliation; that is, in Christ God was reconciling the world to himself, not counting their trespasses against them, and entrusting the message of reconciliation to us. So we are ambassadors for Christ, since God is making his appeal through us; we entreat you on behalf of Christ, be reconciled to God.

What Is Reconciliation?

The word *reconciliation* or *reconcile*, as Paul used it in the Greek (*katallasso, katallage, apokattallasso*), is not derived from any particular word in the Hebrew Scriptures or in Greek religious language. According to theologian Harold Ditmanson: "In classical Greek . . . it denoted a change from a state of enmity to one of friendship, the healing of a quarrel. . . . a radical change occurs in which an intimate and personal relationship is renewed. There is the suggestion of a real friendship, first existing, then broken, and finally restored."[3] When Paul used the word *reconciliation,* he applied a spiritual dimension. Paul described the gospel by using the language of personal relationships. Biblical scholar Ralph Martin adds that "the announcement of reconciliation is *expressible only in personal terms,* whether we recall Christ's obedience to God or the believer's response to all that reconciliation involves as a vital, loving relationship set up with persons always in view."[4] Using the term *reconciliation* acknowledges that there are preexisting barriers to relationships. So reconciliation signals the reconnecting of those who have parted.

Paul uses the term *reconciliation* or *reconcile* only a few times (Romans 5:10-11; 11:15; 2 Corinthians 5:18-19; Ephesians 2:16; and Colossians 1:20, 22). He seems to reserve this word for use as the most powerful way of expressing the meaning of the life, death, and resurrection of Jesus Christ. The coming of Jesus Christ offered the world such a powerful new opportunity "that a new and original word was needed to describe it."[5] The following phrases, when combined, begin to capture its meaning: (1) being put into friendship with God and each other, (2) radical change and transformation of a relationship, and (3) restoration of harmony.

God and the Individual

Paul made it very clear that the reconciliation he was speaking of originated with God: "All this is from God" (2 Corinthians 5:18). We react to God's initiative in reconciliation. All of humanity is invited to respond to God's reaching out to us. The Hebrews often spoke of making peace with God, or atonement (at-one-ment). So the Jews among Paul's readers understood the concept of reconciliation with God. Their struggle was with the use of a "human" Jesus as the mediator. As I mentioned, the Greeks used the word *reconciliation* to describe the result of individuals who had been in opposition to each other becoming friends again. But they did not apply this concept to God.[6] When Paul wrote of being reconciled to God, the Greeks in his readership were being asked to embrace a new concept. So we could say that reconciliation with God through Jesus Christ was often "a stumbling block to Jews and foolishness to Gentiles" (1 Corinthians 1:23).

The process of reconciliation begins when an individual accepts God's invitation to make things right. Paul is clear that we all are in need of this peace with God. In the following two passages, Paul says that we were estranged from God, but through Jesus Christ we can be reconciled.

> For if while we were enemies, we were reconciled to God through the death of his Son, much more surely, having been reconciled, will we be saved by his life. But more than that, we even boast in God through our Lord Jesus Christ, through whom we have now received reconciliation. (Romans 5:10-11)

> And you who were once estranged and hostile in mind, doing evil deeds, he has now reconciled in his fleshly body through death, so as to present you holy and blameless and irreproachable before him—provided that you continue securely established and steadfast in the faith, without shifting from the hope promised by the gospel that you heard, which has been proclaimed to every creature under heaven. I, Paul, became a servant of this gospel. (Colossians 1:21-23)

Paul states that sin caused our relationship with God to become fractured. The death of Jesus was understood as the action that repaired our relationship with God. To be reconciled to God, then, is to move from estrangement to friendship. It means being changed completely. All animosity and bitterness are removed. Reconciliation comes to us from God as a divine gift. Until we are at peace with God, we will not experience life in its fullness. Reconciliation is a process of healing that leads to freedom and liberation. The effect, from God's point of view, is that "everything old has passed away; see, everything has become new!" (2 Corinthians 5:17). When we are reconciled with God, our old life passes away and a new life takes over, propelling us toward wholeness. Through a process of casting off the dysfunction in our emotions, spirit, psyche, and relationships, we become healthy. In this reconciled relationship with God, we find strength to live as new persons, even though our environment and our world often do not change.

God's Desire for Oneness in the Human Family

A healthy relationship with God produces the desire to be at peace with our sisters and brothers in the human family. When we have been truly reconciled with God, we hunger for a restoration to a primitive unity that was spoken into existence at the beginning of human history.

> Then God said: "Let us make humankind in our image, according to our likeness. . . ." So God created humankind in his image, in the image of God he created them; male and female he created them. (Genesis 1:26-27)

According to the Bible, through Adam and Eve flow all persons who have ever existed on this earth. We have a common origin. We are one family. We share the same original gene pool.[7] In other words, if we go back far enough, our family trees will converge. We are also all equal before the Almighty because each of us shares the distinct honor of being created in the very image of God.

The oneness of the human family was further illustrated by the placement of Eden, the original homeland for the first human couple. The borders of Eden were rivers on the continents of Africa and Asia and therefore included the world known to the early Hebrews. This oneness was restated as Noah and his family left the ark: "The sons of Noah who went out of the ark were Shem, Ham, and Japheth. . . . These three were the sons of Noah; and from these the whole earth was peopled" (Genesis 9:18-19). The unity of the human race echoes throughout the Psalms and the writings of the prophets. The fact that this oneness was recorded by the Hebrew writers of the Bible gives further evidence that, even as they developed their own ethnic identity, they recognized that the

Hebrew people belonged to a larger human family.[8] The apostle Paul summed it up in this statement: "From one ancestor [God] made all nations to inhabit the whole earth" (Acts 17:26). I believe that my daughter, Rachel, succinctly captured the essence of this truth when as a small child she declared, "God made a big world so a lot of different people could live in it."

Despite this emphasis on our fundamental oneness throughout the Scriptures, division has often prevailed. Paul's use of the word *reconciliation* referred to the severing of human relations and the widespread hostility among the human family. Paul believed that the death and resurrection of Jesus Christ was a re-creation experience that served as a catalyst for restoring this primitive unity.

> But now in Christ Jesus you who were once far off have been brought near by the blood of Christ. For he is our peace; in his flesh he has made both groups into one and has broken down the dividing wall, that is, the hostility between us. He has abolished the law with its commandments and ordinances, that he might create in himself one new humanity in place of the two, thus making peace, and might reconcile both groups to God in one body through the cross, thus putting to death that hostility through it. (Ephesians 2:13-16; see also vv. 17-22 and Romans 11:13-15)

The "dividing wall" was a reference to the point in the temple where non-Jews, women, and others considered unclean were not allowed access according to Jewish law. Interestingly, Paul wrote to Christians in Ephesus while in prison for breaking that law. He was falsely charged with bringing a Gentile coworker from Ephesus into the temple's inner chamber (Acts 21:27-29). This context must have intensified the symbolism of the "dividing wall" for the Ephesians. Paul was claiming that in the life, death, and resurrection of Jesus Christ the walls of exclusiveness exhibited in temple religion

were broken down. Also about the same time that this passage was written, Jews and Syrians were killing each other
in the streets of Caesarea.[9] The tensions between colonial
Rome and the people who were subject to Rome's rule were
running high. Harold Ditmanson describes the situation as
follows:

> Millions of subjugated people lived under the rule of a
> foreign race. They were always discontented and fre-
> quently rebellious. Economic and political problems
> became so severe that only by means of a rigorous,
> dictatorial regimentation could Roman supremacy be
> maintained. Class hatred, the humiliation of the poor,
> unspeakable cruelty to slaves, and the bloodthirsty
> sports of the amphitheater point to the dark side of the
> Roman character.[10]

The act of reconciliation was meant to break down both
the walls in temple religion and those of societal oppression.

A powerful example of breaking down dividing walls can
be found in the Church of God (Anderson, Indiana), which
began in the 1880s as a reformation movement for Christian
unity. The institution of slavery had not long been abolished,
and it had been replaced by legally enforced segregation. At
the Church of God's Alabama State Campmeeting in 1897,
both African Americans and whites attended the services.
African Americans sat on one side and whites on the other
side. A rope was stretched down the middle aisle in recognition of the legally required segregation. One day, Rev. Lena
Shoffner preached about tearing down the "middle wall of
partition" (Ephesians 2:14 KJV). Some people were so per-
suaded by her message that they took down the rope that
separated the races. Those assembled knelt down together in
prayer—in violation of Alabama state law. That dramatic act
of reconciliation did not go unnoticed by a racist and segregated society.

Church of God historian John W. V. Smith described what

happened as a result of this act of courage: "That night a mob came to the campground in wild fury. They threw dynamite under the boarding house and camp houses and searched out each of the preachers and evangelists, most of whom had already fled into the night." Smith notes that the mob was so outraged by this defiant act of oneness that the next night "the mob followed them to the homes where they had sought refuge, in some cases up to fifteen miles away from the campgrounds."[11] Just as the dividing wall between Jew and Gentile was broken down only after Jesus Christ had suffered on the cross, our attempts at unity may require a similar sacrifice. Reconciliation is costly!

Paul's attempt to reconcile Jews with those outside their faith tradition and cultural understanding was a significant challenge. Although Judaism believed in being reconciled to God, reconciliation of individuals was considered necessary only between Jewish men. This "reconciliation" (*diallassomai* as in Matthew 5:24) was an "in-house" action. Paul expanded this concept to apply to Jew and Gentile by relating it to the individual's reconciliation with God. If Jews and Gentiles were reconciled to God, they were therefore automatically reconciled to each other. In fact, Paul went so far as to say that out of these two groups of people God created "one new humanity" superseding the categories of Jew and Gentile. To follow Jesus Christ was to embrace the restoration of true humanity, the primitive unity. This was the "new creation" (2 Corinthians 5:17). Paul's insights were a result of his own personal transformation. As Samuel Hines said: "[Paul] had personal experience supporting the claim that whole patterns of perception can be changed, so that we see beyond the 'flesh' tags and value people by standards not implied by such labels as race, nationality, class, economic standing, religious rating and a thousand other categories which we use to manipulate and segregate people."[12]

Biblical scholar Fred Burnett was born in Birmingham,

Alabama, in 1944. He grew up during the era of legally enforced segregation. Martin Luther King Jr. and the Southern Christian Leadership Conference came to town in April 1963. To Burnett and his family, King was a Communist and a lawbreaker. On May 3, 1963, the most volatile day of the campaign, Fred Burnett and two of his friends came out of a movie theater in downtown Birmingham and were confronted by the sight of hundreds of African Americans marching two by two. Burnett and his friends made several attempts to interpret these events out of their own reality. First they considered that maybe African Americans were trying to overtake Birmingham just as their families, Police Commissioner Eugene "Bull" Connor, and Governor George Wallace had said. Yet the civil rights workers were marching in an orderly fashion, carrying no guns and doing no looting. Next they considered their assumption that African Americans were always happy, always singing and dancing. Yet the marchers looked very serious and determined. They were singing, but it was a melancholy refrain, "we shall overcome." Finally they decided that at least they could depend on the "fact" that African Americans have smaller brains than whites. But Fred had to ask himself honestly: "Who has the smaller brain, the eight-year-old black girl being hosed or the adult white fireman hosing her?" Fred Burnett reflects: "We were literally confronted by an event of such magnitude, that nothing, at least in my vocabulary and world-view, could make sense out of what I saw! The 'truth' as I had been given it, just didn't fit the event." He eventually accepted Martin Luther King Jr.'s interpretation of the event: the rule of God was breaking into history.

Two years later while Burnett was a sophomore at Anderson University in Indiana, the Selma-to-Montgomery march was taking place in Alabama. The university's president, Robert Reardon, invited students to participate in a sympathy march from the campus to the courthouse in Anderson. Most southern students, as well as most northern students, chose to remain on campus for a prayer meeting. Fred Burnett chose to go on the sympathy march, an action that symbolized the change that had taken place. He says that his body was literally shaking as he marched because "an old worldview was falling, and it was being replaced by a totally new view of existence and who should be in what places in the world." The Birmingham event transformed Burnett's whole perspective on life. [13] Two groups of people, whites and African Americans, were becoming one new humanity. A new creation was emerging. The process of reconciliation was moving forward. It seemed that the ministers of the Southern Christian Leadership Conference were accomplishing their mission "to redeem the soul of America."

Paul's understanding of unity and the need for reconciliation expanded beyond the relationship between Jews and Gentiles. He also recognized that this ministry of reconciliation included breaking down the dividing walls between men and women, slave and free, and all other groups of people who were estranged or separated (Galatians 3:28). Reconciliation was to be applied to concrete human situations. The purpose of reconciliation was (and is) to repair the damage of division and to restore the reality of oneness. Paul's message was oneness, unity—reconciliation.

Jesus—"The Reconciler par Excellence"

Let us take a step back from Paul's theological perspective of reconciliation and examine the source, Jesus—the reconciler par excellence. The perspective of Jesus of Nazareth was shaped by the daily events of life in the context in which he was born and raised. His life began with dramatic events: birth in a barn under scandalous circumstances, visits by poor shepherds from Palestine and rich magi from Asia, and nighttime travel to Africa to find refuge from Herod's threats of murder. We also know that Jesus of Nazareth was a descendant of the Hebrew people. Hebrew heritage found its roots in Asia, Africa, and the indigenous people of Palestine. The family tree of Jesus was no different. It was multicultural and multiracial. Some scholars have declared that Jesus was an Afro-Asiatic Jew.[14] Jesus lived all of his life in Palestine, the land that bridges the continents of Africa and Asia, near the gateway to Europe. At different times in history Palestine has been referred to as West Asia or Northeast Africa.[15]

Not only was Jesus born into a family with a diverse heritage, but he spent most of his days from childhood to adulthood in the province of Galilee, home to many groups of people during the first century. People from Assyria, Babylonia, Egypt, Macedonia, Persia, Rome, and Syria, as well as the Jews, resided there.[16] Religion scholar Roberto W. Pazmiño writes that

> in the first century, Galilee with a population of approximately 350,000 persons had a large slave element and about 100,000 Jews who were largely Hellenized [assimilated into Greek culture]. The primary language was Koine Greek, although Jews spoke Aramaic. Thus the Galilean Jews represented a bilingual community. . . . This region was occupied by a mixed population and had a reputation for racial variety and mixture in and around its borders.[17]

Therefore Jesus spent most of his life in a region that included people from a wide range of cultures, social classes, religions, and languages. Jesus himself probably spoke three languages: Aramaic, Koine Greek, and Hebrew.

During his ministry, Jesus proclaimed the inclusive nature of the gospel: "Then people will come from east and west, from north and south, and will eat in the kingdom of God" (Luke 13:29). The life of Jesus exemplified his teaching. He reached out to people who were not of his cultural background, whether Samaritans, Romans, or indigenous Canaanites. Women traveled with Jesus as part of his entourage and provided the funds for his work. At the crucifixion of Jesus it was an African, Simon of Cyrene, who carried his cross; it was a European, a Roman centurion, who spoke words of faith. Women were the first witnesses to Jesus' resurrection. After his resurrection, Jesus challenged his followers to "go therefore and make disciples of all nations" (Matthew 28:19). From birth to death and in every moment between, Jesus of Nazareth radiated a spirit of inclusiveness and reconciliation.[18]

Perhaps the most compelling act of reconciliation that Jesus initiated in his ministry was his invitation for people who were considered sinners and outcasts in society to join him at the dinner table.[19] This action was quite controversial, as the response of some Pharisees indicated: "Why does he eat with tax collectors and sinners?" (Mark 2:15-16). Eating a meal with someone in first-century Palestine suggested that you had accepted that person as your friend. Jesus intentionally crossed the boundaries established by society and created relationships with those who were devalued by the community. He shared food and drink with women, Samaritans, poor people, diseased individuals, and many others— and he did it in public! He taught about reconciliation by acting it out in the presence of those who desired it most. Everyone was welcome at the table. God came in Jesus Christ "to do an on-site job of reconciliation."[20]

Not only did Jesus share meals with people whom society refused to embrace; he physically touched individuals no one else would touch. He touched the diseased skin of lepers. In the middle of synagogue worship, he touched a woman who had been bent over for eighteen years. He touched people who were demon-possessed. Jesus even touched people who had died. He also felt no discomfort when people touched him. Jesus was touched by a woman with an issue of blood. On another occasion he was touched by a "sinful" woman who was overwhelmed by his ministry of inclusion.

She began by washing Jesus' feet with her tears and drying them with her hair. As if that was not enough, she then kissed and anointed his feet. All of this touching was considered inappropriate for a rabbi and abhorred by many.

I served for a few years in a ministry that fed homeless people in Washington, D.C. The Third Street Church of God and One Ministries hosted a breakfast Monday through Friday, every week of the year, that often fed more than three hundred people. Many people came there from sleeping in a shelter or on the streets of downtown Washington to eat breakfast with us. The morning began with a worship service that included a time for individuals to come forward for prayer. We always laid a hand on each person or put an arm around someone. That human touch in the midst of inhumane circumstances powerfully affected the lives of many who came. One woman came regularly and wanted to show her affection by giving a kiss on the cheek. She often brought with her a strong smell from a lack of bathing and a tendency to sleep in urine-drenched doorways. One of my coworkers developed a case of ringworm from her kiss. My faith in Jesus was tested every time she greeted me with a "God bless you" and a kiss. But I knew my discomfort and health concerns were nothing in comparison to her need to feel and express love.

Jesus did not stop with eating and touching; he further broke social and religious taboos by talking about faith with women, Samaritans, Gentiles, and poor folks. These actions were considered to be inappropriate and a waste of time, but Jesus felt that they were a significant part of his mission that was meant for all people. Jesus talked about faith, for example, with a woman from Samaria, a Canaanite woman, Martha of Bethany, Mary of Bethany, and Mary Magdalene. In his eating, touching, and talking, he set people free. Jesus reconciled individuals, one by one, into a relationship with

God and with each other. Jesus of Nazareth was the reconciler par excellence.

The Early Church as a Model

When Jesus was executed on a Roman cross, the strategy
for broad societal reconciliation began to reveal itself. The
first crack in the Jewish-Roman wall of hostility was observed when a Roman guard at the cross said, "Truly this man
was God's Son!" (Mark 15:39). This member of colonial
Rome's occupying police force saw past an oppressed Jewish
"criminal" and recognized a profound mystery. The Roman
military man's recognition of the significance of Jesus was
just a glimmer of things to come. For when Jesus was crucified, the stage was being set for the greatest act of reconciliation in the history of the human family. No Roman cross, no
Roman seal on Jesus' grave, no show of military force around
the tomb could stop God Almighty from raising Jesus from
the dead and initiating the era of reconciliation. The Resurrection was God's endorsement of all that Jesus had modeled
in his life. The Gospel writer Luke had to write an entire
second volume, the Acts of the Apostles, to record how
quickly this movement of reconciliation spread throughout
society.

This gospel of reconciliation reached out to the powerless
in society by transforming the lives of Samaritans, beggars,
and others marginalized by society. The early church followed Jesus' lead in reinterpreting the role of women by
giving them leadership as evangelists, preachers, prophets,
deacons, and apostles. In Paul's seminal work, the Book of
Romans, he identifies sixteen women who served with him
in the ministry of the gospel. Women like Mary, Lydia, Prisca,
Chloe, Nympha, Apphia, Euodia, Syntyche, Philip's four
daughters, Phoebe, and Junia were among those whom God
called and the church ordained.[21] The message of reconciliation also reached out to the powerful: an Ethiopian treasury

official was baptized; Roman military officers were filled
with the Holy Spirit; Roman jailers got saved; and the apostle
Paul was on his way to Rome to witness to Caesar himself.
In some places, rich and poor folks of faith even began living
in community and holding all things in common. Also, congregations with economic surplus supported those located
in areas of poverty.

Jews, Greeks, Romans, Africans, Asians, Samaritans, and
others were finding common ground in the faith of Jesus. It
started at Pentecost and continued with the founding of
multicultural congregations. The Antioch congregation was
the crowning jewel of the early church's ministry, which
extended from Palestine into Africa, Asia, and Europe. "Now
in the church at Antioch there were prophets and teachers:
Barnabas, Simeon who was called Niger, Lucius of Cyrene,
Manaen a member of the court of Herod the ruler, and Saul"
(Acts 13:1). Simeon and Lucius were from Africa, Barnabas
and Saul were Jews, and Manaen may have been a European.
Although such a leadership team is highly unusual in our
day, the reader of Acts is given no special notice that this was
an experiment in reconciliation. The normative nature of
such ministry is also confirmed by what is not stated in the
New Testament. For example, the three most important leaders in the formation of the Corinthian church in Europe were
Peter, Paul, and Apollos. Peter was from Palestine, Paul was
born in Asia, and Apollos was born in Africa, but the fact that
a Palestinian Jew, an Asian, and an African provided leadership in this European church was never mentioned. Although first-century Christians were aware of ethnic and
cultural distinctions, it was one's membership in the human
race that prompted an invitation to join the community of
Jesus Christ.[22]

The ministry of reconciliation was set loose in the world
through Jesus' resurrection, and it radically transformed individual lives and institutional structures. The life, death,

and resurrection of Jesus Christ ushered in new possibilities for peace, new power for societal transformation, and new passion for reconciliation. Biblical scholar Craig S. Keener notes that Christians "formed the only bridge between Jews and Gentiles and had few allies in challenging class (slave versus free) and gender prejudices."[23] The message of reconciliation can be summed up in Paul's proclamation that "there is no longer Jew or Greek, there is no longer slave or free, there is no longer male or female, for all of you are one in Christ Jesus" (Galatians 3:28; see also Romans 10:12; 1 Corinthians 12:13; Ephesians 2:11-16; Colossians 3:11). As a changed people with changed relationships, the early followers of Jesus were changing the world.

Our Call Today

Our appraisal of modern Christianity in chapter 3 leads to this question: Have we departed from the ministry of Jesus and the example of the early church? If we have arrived at a place where unity is unique and division is the norm, then we have created a faith understanding rooted in separation rather than oneness. The question we need to ask is this: How can we revive the early church's inclusive nature? Addressing separation as it exists in our church life will involve more than challenging individuals. Many congregations, denominations, academic institutions, para-church organizations, and other associations claiming to be Christian are far from modeling the inclusive nature of God. We need once again to hear and answer the call to be "ambassadors of Christ" for reconciliation (2 Corinthians 5:20).

An ambassador is someone who represents a ruler or a nation and speaks on behalf of whomever he is representing. An ambassador has no message of her own, only that of the one whom she represents. As Christ's ambassadors we speak and act on behalf of God. We do not speak for ourselves; we speak the message of God—reconciliation. God's one-item agenda becomes our agenda. As religion professor Doris Donnelly writes:

> When Paul passes the mantle of ambassadorial rank to each of us, we may surmise two things: First, that God's intention for the world is unity, and second, that the mission to gather the world as one which was begun by Jesus was left incomplete by him. That mission was delegated to the community of believers gathered in his name.
>
> Each of us is an ambassador in the service of a leader who deputizes us to spread news of peace, restoration, and collaboration to a world sorely in need of this news. There are few things about which God is more persistent than this—that each of us engage in this ministry of reconciliation and bring it to completion. It is nothing less than our meaning, our historical destiny, and our corporate identity.[24]

As ambassadors of reconciliation, we are called to act on behalf of God to remove barriers to harmonious relationships. We struggle against racism, sexism, classism, homophobia, and all things that produce division. We grapple with hatred, prejudice, jealousy, gossip, and the like. At the same time, we strive for peace, justice, equality, and integrity. We practice, and encourage in others, love, joy, hope, and faith. It is an honor and privilege to be God's ambassadors of reconciliation. Simply stated, to be a Christian, by definition, is to be involved in the ministry of reconciliation. If reconciliation is God's one-item agenda, then we must rediscover that power exhibited by the early church that transformed individuals and society. The road to recovering our oneness may be paved with struggle, but as followers of Jesus Christ we must respond to the call to take up our cross and proclaim reconciliation with our words and actions, no matter what the cost. God's one-item agenda is our only hope!

Questions for Discussion

1. After reading this chapter, how would you define *reconciliation?*

2. Do you agree that reconciliation is God's one-item agenda? Why or why not?

3. What does it mean to be reconciled to God? How have you experienced this in your life?

4. Given the Bible's emphasis on God's desire for oneness, why do you think we are so far from achieving this ideal? What will it take to get closer to God's desire for unity? What can we do?

5. Identify the various ways that Jesus practiced reconciliation in first-century Palestine. How can we become more like Jesus in our individual lives and in the life of our church community?

6. What in this chapter provided the most compelling reason for you to make reconciliation a priority? Explain.

7. Describe the role of an ambassador of reconciliation. Can you see yourself in that role? If so, in what ways? If not, why not?

5

A Reconciliation Mind-Set

During the 1960s, one of the most imposing figures in the United States was George Wallace, governor of the state of Alabama. He was a symbol of America's apartheid: legally enforced segregation in southern states. Governor Wallace's motto was "Segregation now! Segregation tomorrow! Segregation forever!"[1] In 1965, he ordered state troopers to stop civil rights marchers from crossing the Edmund Pettis Bridge in Selma, Alabama. This was the route that led from Selma to Montgomery, the state capital. When the marchers attempted to cross the bridge, they were met with billy clubs and tear gas. It was one of the most brutal scenes of the civil rights movement and came to be known as Bloody Sunday. The march was eventually completed under court-ordered federal protection and led to one of the most important victories of the civil rights movement, the passage of the Voting Rights Act. George Wallace, a Methodist layperson, agreed to meet with the marchers when they arrived in Montgomery. (He did this only at the request of Alabama's Methodist bishop.) Civil rights activist Joseph Lowery writes of that meeting: "I advised him, as a Methodist preacher to a Methodist layman, that God would hold him accountable for his hateful words which others transformed into hateful deeds."[2]

In March 1995, many of the marchers retraced their steps to commemorate the thirtieth anniversary of this significant juncture in U.S. history. But this time the marchers received an unexpected request. George Wallace asked to greet them when they arrived in Montgomery. Joseph Lowery reflects on this turn of events: "Since Wallace had nothing to gain politically, I welcomed his offer of reconciliation.... I thanked George Wallace for his act of courtesy. Marchers applauded his welcome. We could not, would not, deny him an act of repentance. We serve a God who makes the crooked places straight. God makes the desert bloom and the lion lie down with the lamb. There was an air of regeneration and reconciliation in those moments! Isn't that what the world needs now? I think so!"[3]

I begin the chapter with this incident because, unless we believe that reconciliation is possible, there is no reason to pursue it. Civil rights leader Jesse Jackson sees the repentant George Wallace as "a symbol for those Americans trapped in a racist society who want to change their and the society's ways."[4] We need symbols of hope to move us forward in this enterprise of coming together. The biblical mandate articulated in the preceding chapter gives us our marching orders. Yet we must come to the task of relational peacemaking with certain attitudes and ways of thinking. We need a reconciliation mind-set. So in this chapter and the next, I highlight some basic principles for reconciliation. Then in chapters 7–9, I examine a process for moving toward this desired intent.[5] I contend that reconciliation is possible and that it begins with self-examination; it is holistic and consistent; it requires a persistent resolve; and it is centered in relationships.

Reconciliation Begins with Self-Examination

Simply believing that reconciliation is possible is not enough. As God's instruments for creating unity, we must examine ourselves to discover if anything within us inhibits reconciliation. Some of us may see no bigotry in our own lives. When I was in college, I believed that I was free from racism. I eventually discovered that my belief was based on ill-founded optimism. The revelation came during my senior year. There was a certain young white woman whom I found attractive, and I planned to ask her out on a date. One day I happened to see her in the company of two African American men. Sometime later I saw her again and realized that the previous attraction was gone. As I reflected on the situation, I came to the conclusion that my interest had subsided at the same time I saw her accompanied by African American men. I had fallen prey to an old prejudice perpetrated by slave masters: African American men are sexual animals, and any white woman who associates with a black man is immoral and therefore defiled. I had to recognize and admit that I was not without prejudice.

We may have reasons for avoiding self-examination. If someone suggests that we are prejudiced, do we simply disregard his or her comments as an ill-informed attempt to make us feel guilty? Rather than immediately denying the charges, perhaps we should examine our attitudes to discover whether we are harboring prejudice. Many years ago when I worked at a shelter for runaway youth, I had the responsibility of escorting to the door a young woman who had been discharged for hitting a counselor. The woman, of a different race from mine, called me a bigot for removing her from the premises. Though I was quite sure that this was not the reason for her expulsion, I was bothered by the accusation of prejudice. I wanted to tell her how wrong she was about my character. After the encounter, I began to ponder why her comment had irritated me so much. I used this as an opportunity for self-examination. If I had such a need to defend myself against her charge of bigotry, maybe I was not as unbiased as I had believed. Taking a candid look at ourselves means considering our own prejudices.

In what ways can we become more sensitive and accepting of others? We may want to ask others to help us in this task of self-analysis.

We must also be clear about how bigotry affects our relationships and our understanding of the world. Is every unpleasant encounter between people of different races due to racism? Is every man a sexist? Do all middle-class people hold classist views? Perhaps the young woman in the episode just described could have better identified her role in the discharge from the facility if she had asked whether her choice to hit a counselor brought consequences that were not caused by bias. (Such an acknowledgment would not, of course, dismiss the fact that she was also facing societal barriers as a poor woman of color.)

Another area that warrants attention is our motivation. Are we trying to immerse ourselves in another culture to escape our guilt, or are we trying to build mutually fulfilling relationships? If we are members of the group in power, are we willing to address sexism, racism, classism, and other forms of bigotry within our "own group," or does that effort seem less attractive than working with the "victims" of oppression? As imperfect human beings, how do we maintain a godly attitude as we embody the ministry of reconciliation? Such questions invite constructive criticism and provide opportunities for growth. I believe we must be willing to struggle with such questions even when the answers are not clear-cut.

Reconciliation Is Holistic and Consistent

Self-examination can help ensure that our actions as reconcilers are holistic and consistent. As I stated in the introduction, reconciliation must be understood and practiced broadly. People who fight against racism but ignore sexism are undermining their own best efforts. Individuals who struggle for gender equality but ignore class dynamics are

limiting their potential to create substantive change. A holistic approach to racism also reminds us that race in the United
States has never been an issue simply between blacks and
whites. In fact, Native Americans have struggled the longest
with "white racism." Many Asians have experienced their
first bitter taste of racism in the United States. People who
define themselves from a cultural perspective often learn
upon arrival in the United States that they are also members
of "a race." Race and culture do intersect. If one studies
poverty in the United States, it becomes apparent that race
and class dynamics also cross paths.

Approaching reconciliation holistically allows the issues
that divide us to be considered together. In fact, the very act
of examining issues simultaneously allows new solutions to
emerge. Theologian Eldin Villafañe likens reconciliation to
jazz musicians' use of fusion to create new music. He writes
that "Latin Jazz" is "the fusion of Afro-Cuban, jazz, blues,
and other music influences. . . . Not only Hispanics listen
to Latin Jazz—it's now a crossover, as African Americans
and Anglos enjoy it, too." Villafañe sees this fusion of
ethnomusical strands into Latin Jazz as "celebrating a true
harmony of the contributions of people of all colors . . . [and
as] a prophetic challenge to the church to be the 'space' where
the presence and contribution of believers of all colors could
be seen as 'light' and could be savored as 'salt' in a broken
world."[6] Reconciliation efforts need to create a space where
all struggles against injustice fuse together in fresh experiments of community. Hopes for lasting reconciliation will be
dashed if efforts to create a just society and more unified
community are isolated from each other. As Martin Luther
King Jr. often proclaimed, "Injustice anywhere is a threat to
justice everywhere."[7]

The reconciler must also be consistent in her or his commitment to repairing broken relationships. How easy it is to
be a public reconciler and a private dictator. But ignoring our

own unreconciled private relationships contradicts our most eloquent arguments for harmony and, in fact, borders on hypocrisy. It is often harder to reconcile relationships with our spouses, children, or other family members than it is to address reconciliation in society at large. Yet the same skills are required both at home and in our communities. Although we cannot guarantee that our efforts will bring success in the private or public realm, we can make every effort to pursue reconciliation in all spheres of life.

Reconciliation Requires Persistent Resolve

When working for reconciliation, one also needs a persistent resolve. In other words, we must be patient! It took us a long time to get into the mess we are in; therefore, it may take a long time to get out of it. Racism, sexism, classism, and other "isms" that divide us are deeply entrenched in the United States.[8] The genocide of Native Americans, the enslavement of Africans, the domination of women, and the disenfranchisement of the poor—all were part of the formation of the United States. Reversing formative acts and replacing them with the values of reconciliation are not easily accomplished, but we cannot allow this difficulty to inhibit our resolve. It is through persistence that change in structures, cultures, and individuals is attained.

Another reason for persistence is that the theme of reconciliation has only recently been reemphasized. Although it was the guiding message of the early church and greatly influenced first-century society, it was lost somewhere along the way. According to theologian Harold Ditmanson, reconciliation, as a theological concept, was not studied by theologians during most of the history of the church. He writes: "It is one of a small family of words used by Paul for the central reality of Christian faith and life. Yet the aptness and power of the idea of reconciliation seem not to have been recognized until the nineteenth century." Ditmanson adds that "it is more probable that the strongly personalistic quality of the reconciliation theme was not considered important during the period between Paul and the nineteenth century."[9]

Had reconciliation been considered important "between Paul and the nineteenth century," perhaps more Christians would have spoken prophetically against slavery, colonialism, and numerous other injustices. Instead, much of the organized church undergirded and supported slavery, economic injustice, the slaughter of indigenous peoples, and the oppression of women by providing a theological rationale. These tragic historical choices confirm our need for a persistent resolve. We must change the way the church has thought about the gospel and pursued its mission for centuries. Reconciliation means doing business in a new way, as we shall see in chapters 7–9.

Not only have reconciliation themes recently been revived in theological discussions, but the message of reconciliation is now being preached more often. Urban leader Sethard Beverly believes that the interest in reconciliation that has been recently rekindled among "evangelical" Christians originated with the ministry of Samuel G. Hines, "who began expounding and disseminating the neglected message in the early 1960s."[10] Given that the renaissance of reconciliation in theology and preaching are so recent, the current momentum could be lost without perseverance.

Sexism, classism, and racism are alive and well. People and communities are experiencing the effects of bigotry even as you read this. We are dealing with a well-entrenched present reality. So another reason for patience and long-suffering is that the effects of division are still evident and strong. Racial reconciler Glen Kehrein illustrates this when he writes:

> When [we] whites come into a black community wanting to right the wrongs of the past, our attitude is

usually, "I'm a good guy; you can trust me." Then we
confront anger and hostility, and we are bewildered. As
white people, we don't often personally experience the
anger bred by oppression because most interaction with
blacks is on our turf—at work or a sporting event—
where whites are in a majority; in those settings, hostility is well hidden. But when whites come into the turf
of those who feel oppressed, angry, and alienated, those
feelings will not be hidden.

Though whites may desire involvement in the inner
city, when black people begin to question our motives
or confront us with what they see as racism, our response is often, "I didn't come here to subject myself to
this." Because we have the option to pull out whenever
we want to, it's tempting to do so.

There are no simple answers, but there is a simple
word: time. . . .

When whites, new to cross-cultural ministry, start to
experience conflict with blacks, they usually are critical
of the other person while justifying their own reactions.
. . . Sometimes a white person tells me, "I just don't
know if it's worth it. I'm not sure I want to stick with
this."[11]

All of us must determine that it is worth it. All of us will
need a persistent faith. This is true for all of us in any
endeavor at unity. Longevity of commitment, rooted in a
persistent resolve, demonstrates our true intentions to be
ambassadors of reconciliation. Persistent faith leads to consistent practice.

We also need to be persistent in the face of criticism from
our own group. People of color who embrace reconciliation
may be charged with "selling out" their own people. Women
who work for reconciliation are sometimes thought to be
compromising their feminism. Low-income folks who seek
reconciliation with persons who are rich may be thought of
as "wannabes." Men who work for reconciliation may be
considered weak. Rich people who want reconciliation may

be charged with "slumming it." Whites may be challenged because they are seeking to change a system that benefits them. While we are called to persist in this journey of reconciliation, some situations are out of our control. We cannot force a person or group to engage in a process that leads to restored relationships. We must accept and respect persons who make the choice not to participate. I believe that there are no "irreconcilable differences" in God's realm, but within the world of human relationships we face limitations. So we persevere in the Spirit through prayer and the faith that brings hope. What has often seemed impossible has occurred in God's time.

Reconciliation Is Centered in Relationships

Though it may seem obvious, another important principle is that reconciliation is centered in relationships. By definition, reconciliation is relational: first with God, then with each other. Reconciliation does not automatically happen because we preach it, discuss it, or write books about it (such as this one). Reconciliation is accomplished when we live it out in relation to each other. We must never underestimate the power of reconciled relationships. Strong relationships can be forged through honest dialogue. Without a shared understanding of the world-views, perceptions about life, and theological perspectives that each of us brings to the table, attempts to encourage unity are doomed. We therefore need to move beyond superficial attempts to build relationships.

Some years ago Kay James, an African American official in the administration of President George Bush, joined a weekly women's Bible study at a white church. Every year the women and their families took a trip to Myrtle Beach, South Carolina. Throughout the year the women would recount stories from previous trips. When it came time to go, Kay James and her family were not invited. After the other women and their families returned from the trip, James asked why she and her family had not been invited. This is how she relates their explanation: "An uncomfortable silence fell upon the room. 'Well, Kay, we just felt that—well, you know that there aren't very many black people at Myrtle Beach . . . and we just thought you would be uncomfortable.' They were concerned about *us?* Didn't they see the irony?" James gave this reply: "I guess I thought that if we wouldn't be accepted at a certain vacation spot, that you would choose another one rather than leave us out."[12] Kay James's experience demonstrates that, short of genuine reconciliation, no matter what place you achieve in society, you cannot escape the effects of injustice. More important, though, her experience strongly reinforces the concept that reconciliation requires more of relationships than just being in the same room studying the Bible.

Kay James had been able to forge relationships that allowed her to challenge the racism of her fellow Bible study group members, but how do people who do not come in contact with each other reconcile? The challenge then is to find creative ways to bring people together so that relationships can have a chance to blossom. Samuel Hines felt called to respond to this challenge when he moved to Washington, D.C., to become the pastor of the Third Street Church of God. As Hines traveled the twelve blocks that separated his congregation's neighborhood from the United States Capitol, he observed the disparity between the powerless and the powerful. He declared, "God gave me one word when I came and that word was reconciliation."[13] Hines tried many approaches in his pursuit of reconciliation in the nation's capital.

One of his experiments was hosting a weekly prayer breakfast in the basement of his church for a small group of religious and political leaders. One fall morning, an individual at this prayer breakfast left the building with a cup of coffee in hand and ran into a homeless man who was an unemployed carpenter. The man asked if he could get some coffee in the church. He went in and was served a full breakfast. He let his friends know about the breakfast. Soon hundreds of people from the neighborhood, the shelters, and the streets were coming to Third Street Church of God for breakfast, prayer, and worship five days a week. That morning meal became a time when the powerful and the powerless could meet and build relationships. As Samuel Hines described it: "We sing 'Jesus Loves Me' during the service and everybody hugs somebody. You should just see who's hugging who! . . . It's an exciting and rewarding ministry. I'm the most excited man in the world! After seeing a Supreme Court justice hug and fellowship with a street man of twenty years in the name of Christ, who wouldn't be?"[14]

Centering reconciliation in relationships is not negotiable. As stated in chapter 4, the word *reconciliation* literally means becoming friends. Perhaps one of the strongest statements of friendship found in the Bible is Ruth's pledge of commitment to her mother-in-law, Naomi. She exclaimed: "Where you go, I will go; where you lodge, I will lodge; your people shall be my people, and your God my God" (Ruth 1:16). My wife, Karen, and I have this reference inscribed on the inside of our wedding rings as a reminder of what our marriage vows mean. Perhaps each of us needs to inscribe this verse on our hearts and minds if we seek to build reconciled relationships that last. The words of Ruth powerfully describe the depth of relationship needed for reconciliation to be experienced in its fullness.

A reconciliation mind-set is essential for our journey down the road of reconnecting severed relationships. First we must believe that unity is possible. We also need to adopt the discipline of self-examination to ensure that our own attitudes do not sabotage efforts for harmony. This includes pursuing reconciliation in ways that are consistent and holistic. We can see the light at the end of the tunnel in our journey toward peace if we have a strong and persistent resolve. Finally, reconciliation is centered in relationships. In the next chapter I discuss ways to make these relationships empowering.

Questions for Discussion

1. Do you believe that reconciliation is possible? Why or why not?

2. Do you agree that self-examination is important for the reconciler? Suggest some strategies for accomplishing this task.

3. Describe how the various "isms" intersect with each other. Is it possible to address sexism, racism, and classism effectively at the same time? If so, how?

4. Do you agree with the author that our commitment to reconciliation must express itself in both the public and private realms of our lives? Elaborate on your reasons. If someone is going through a divorce or is at odds with family members, should this limit his or her involvement in public acts of reconciliation? If so, when? If not, why?

5. Why do we need persistence in the work of reconciliation? How do we develop the ability to stay the course for the long haul?

6. If reconciliation is centered in relationships, then what should be our priorities in preparing to serve God as reconcilers? What skills should we seek to develop?

7. In this chapter, what caught your attention in a fresh way? How are you going to apply that insight?

6

Empowering Relationships

A few years ago I was asked to preach to an Anglo congregation that shared its building with a Spanish-speaking congregation. Because I was coming to speak about cross-cultural ministry, the Anglo pastor invited the Hispanic congregation to worship with the English-speaking congregation. He suggested that I give a brief summary of my sermon at the beginning of the message. The Latino pastor would translate this summary for the members of his congregation who could not understand English. In this way they could get a sense of the content, even though I do not speak Spanish. Then I was to preach, unhindered, in English so that the Anglo congregation would not be distracted by constant pauses for interpretation.

This scenario posed several problems. The first was that my sermon was called "Crossing Boundaries, Creating Relationships." If the sermon were preached in English, with only a short summary provided for the Hispanic congregation, I would be contradicting the central point of my sermon. So I decided to preach my sermon and have the Latino pastor serve as translator for the entire message. This created a second problem: my sermon would now be twice as long. Also, when I asked for tips on how to speak in a way that would make it easier for translation, the Hispanic pastor

suggested I speak in short sentences, pausing for the interpretation. To accommodate this change, I needed to set aside
my sermon manuscript. Nervous and unaccustomed to the
frequent pauses, I began preaching and waiting for my co-
messenger to translate the sermon into Spanish. After a few
minutes, our timing began to mesh, and it was a wonderful
experience.

I was completely dependent on the Latino pastor for communicating to the members who spoke only Spanish. In fact,
at one point in the sermon, I got a bigger laugh from the
Spanish congregation than I was expecting. I was comparing
a craving for Good News to a craving for chocolate ice cream.
I went on and on about how if I find a place that serves good
chocolate ice cream, I will inform all my friends. Rather than
following me in this repetition, the Hispanic pastor invited
everybody to join me after the service for a trip to the ice
cream shop. I did not discover his humorous "addition" to
the sermon until the service ended. I had no choice but to
trust him. God has created us to need each other. Reconciliation is centered in relationships that empower all parties
involved. Therefore, as we shall discover in this chapter,
reconciliation takes place between equals who acknowledge
their need for each other; it sets people free; it includes all
voices and viewpoints; and it involves taking the risk of
trusting.

Reconciliation Occurs between Equals

Reconciled relationships can occur only when each individual believes and perceives that he or she is an equal
partner and in need of the other. There is no room for relationships between groups of people where, because of arrogance, assimilation, or tokenism, one group is defined as
inferior and the other as superior. Sometimes inequality
manifests itself in our perception and use of power in our
interactions with other people. One person can approach a

relationship with the idea that it is based on equality, while the other person may feel she or he is either superior or inferior. This happens more often than we expect in relationships across class, gender, and racial lines. Unless we can move beyond these perceptions, we will not discover and experience the equality needed for reconciliation. Besides, equality is good for our health. In their book *Soul Theology*, Nicholas Cooper-Lewter and Henry Mitchell state that "when males accept equality, they are relieved of the need to be all-competent and without vulnerability. They can release tears and seek their goals through healthy effort rather than deadly overloads. The gap between male and female life expectancies can be narrowed and the percentage of widows reduced."[1]

In addition to promoting our equality, we need to believe that we do need each other. Martin Luther King Jr. often spoke of our interdependence: "We are tied together in the single garment of destiny, caught in an inescapable network of mutuality. And whatever affects one directly affects all indirectly. For some strange reason I can never be what I want to be until you are what you ought to be. And you can never be what you ought to be until I am what I ought to be. This is the way God's universe is made; this is the way it is structured."[2] In chapter 4 we clearly established that, from the very beginning, the biblical vision was one of the unity of the human family. Jesus came to help humanity rediscover this important theme of human interconnectedness and interdependence. When we seek to unite the human family, we attempt to make visible that which already exists spiritually through the Creation and through the fellowship of Jesus Christ. Although we cannot create unity, we can affirm its existence and point to its power. We must believe that this ancient unity is real if we expect to remain empowered in our efforts to mend relationships. Until we understand the value of interdependence and relate to each other as equals, reconciliation will not be realized.

Reconciliation Sets People Free

We will not come to the table as equals who need each other until we are all free.[3] In fact, liberation is the prerequisite for reconciliation.[4] The reconciliation we proclaim must set people free, or it is not the reconciliation practiced by Jesus and proclaimed by Paul. That means we must be willing to take the side of the oppressed. South African bishop Desmond M. Tutu reminds us that "true reconciliation occurs when we confront people with the demands of the gospel of Jesus Christ for justice and peace and compassion and caring. It means taking sides on behalf of the weak and the downtrodden, the voiceless ones. We cannot be neutral in situations of injustice and oppression and exploitation."[5] This is perhaps the point where many attempts at relational bridge building fall short. Reconciliation is not just getting along with each other. It is a radical transformation in the way we relate to each other within society. Our efforts at weaving relationships together need to be interwoven with opportunities for setting people free.

In chapter 3 I stated that if we are to discover true reconciliation we must answer the question "Which Jesus is the real Jesus?" When John the Baptist sent his disciples to ask Jesus of Nazareth how John could be sure that he was the one, Jesus replied:

> Go and tell John what you have seen and heard: the blind receive their sight, the lame walk, the lepers are cleansed, the deaf hear, the dead are raised, and the poor have good news brought to them. And blessed is anyone who takes no offense at me. (Luke 7:22-23; cf. Matthew 11:4-6)

We find Jesus of Nazareth pursuing liberation and reconciliation amid the powerless and marginalized. If we claim to follow *the real Jesus*, our reconciliation work will set individuals free, one by one, and dismantle the systems of injustice that oppress people. Our liberation efforts will also include freeing those who are imprisoned by their need to be in control or feel superior (even if they have never perceived their need). Those in power also need liberation. Reconciliation requires that we are committed to setting *all* people free—spiritually, emotionally, psychologically, socially, and physically. Reconciliation and liberation are intertwined because, as theologian J. Deotis Roberts has declared, "Christ is at once the Liberator and Reconciler."[6]

Reconciliation Includes All Voices and Viewpoints

In order to sustain reconciled relationships that are based on equality and freedom, all voices must be included, valued, and encouraged. We need to learn to listen as individuals from outside of our realm of comprehension describe their life experiences. Peace activist Máiread Maguire addresses this challenge when she speaks about the struggle in her home of Northern Ireland: "We really have people from different cultures, who have not physically been separated but who, in many ways, have been kept apart down through history. We are speaking different languages. It is as if we are culturally deaf in one ear, and cannot hear what the other culture is saying."[7] We can understand where others are coming from only when we hear their voices and learn of their viewpoints. Reconciliation calls us to seek such opportunities.

I call this attempt to comprehend the experience of others "multicultural fluency."[8] Fluency in understanding life from multiple perspectives counters the pervasive effects of separation. This is extremely important for those of us who have been raised in culturally or economically isolated urban, suburban, or rural areas. We need to hear the stories of people who differ from us culturally, racially, and economically. Men and women must truly seek to hear each other's stories. We need to learn to hear the voices of all our brothers and sisters in the human family. To accomplish this, "those who have power in society (or the church), and thereby already have a voice, will need to listen more."[9] The voiceless may need to be invited into the conversation if they have previously been marginalized or tokenized in attempts at dialogue.

How do we become multiculturally fluent? It happens as our life intersects and interconnects with the lives of others, as we leave our comfort zones and, for extended periods, relate to people whose lives differ from our own. Our multicultural vocabulary increases as we listen to and live with people from a diversity of settings. Transformation ensues when we are mentored by persons who are different from us. It is particularly important for men to be mentored by women and for whites to be mentored by people of color. Our viewpoints and perceptions are radically altered when we leave our places of comfort and experience fresh perspectives. It is important for us to gain some ability to see life through the eyes of others.

Another way we become multiculturally fluent is by studying history from a variety of perspectives. Such an approach to history may cause us to ask questions: Did Columbus discover or invade America? Given that many Native American nations viewed land as common property, unable to be bought and sold, did the Dutch buy or steal Manhattan? Was George Washington the father of freedom or a hypocritical slave owner? After the verdicts in the Rodney King case, did Los Angeles erupt in riots or a rebellion? By reading widely, we gain the ability to interact with multiple perspectives of history and strengthen our multicultural fluency for the present. By reading works penned by authors who come from different racial, cultural, and socioeconomic settings or are of the opposite gender, we stay in touch with worlds outside our own. All of this helps us to hear more accurately the viewpoints of others.[10]

Reconciliation means intentionally including all voices and viewpoints in the process. Yet it is more than just listening to traditionally unheard voices. It also means including women, people of color, the poor, and other marginalized people in actually fashioning the decisions and determining the consequences of our life together. Eric H. F. Law, a consultant on multicultural leadership, has developed a process he calls "Mutual Invitation" to facilitate this commitment to include all voices. The group facilitator or leader begins a discussion by sharing his view on the issue at hand. Then the facilitator invites another member of the group to share. After that person has shared, she chooses the next person. This process continues until everyone has had an opportunity to speak. If someone does not want to offer a comment, he can pass, but he still selects the next person to speak. Comments are interjected only after an invitation to speak. This process allows each person to have both an opportunity to speak and the power to invite someone else into the process. "Experts," "powerful people," "dignitaries," "important officials," even the president of the United States—all follow the process and wait to be invited to speak (even if that means going last). If future meetings are to be held, the facilitator invites someone else to start the process at the next meeting (even subsequent leaders are chosen through the Mutual Invitation process).[11] This process greatly enhances the possibility that everyone's voice will be heard.

In our effort to understand the perspective of others, we must remember that, although we can empathize, we are not the other person. As we listen, we should resist the temptation to believe that we can ever *fully* know what it is like to be another person or part of a group other than our own. While attending seminary, I often filled the pulpit for a nearby congregation that was without a pastor. When my name was suggested as a potential part-time pastor, a leader in this congregation spoke against the suggestion because, in his words, "I had a personal problem." I soon learned that my personal problem was my fiancée, Karen. I was white, and my fiancée (now my wife) was black. Our different responses to this situation illustrated that I could not fully understand her feelings. I suggested to Karen that we should just consider this church leader a "racist jerk." She explained that I could get rid of her and be found worthy by this individual. She could not change who she was; therefore, he would always consider her a "problem." While I could intellectualize this situation, it was deeply hurtful to Karen in a way I could not understand. Our life experiences affected our responses.

It is important, as we listen to the voices of others, that we acknowledge our inability fully to understand the experience of any other person.[12] Yet despite the limitations, there is much we can learn to understand and appreciate about others whose life journey, at first glance, may seem quite dissimilar. We will not become experts, but we can become fluent in the experiences of others. Listening to Karen's response in the above situation broadened my "fluency" regarding her experience, increased my sensitivity, and strengthened our ability to connect within a relationship. Creating opportunities for hearing the voices and viewpoints of those with whom we seldom rub shoulders greatly increases our multicultural fluency. Furthermore, true reconciliation is impossible if everyone does not feel included.

Reconciliation Involves the Risk of Trusting

Only when there is trust will the process of reconciliation include all voices and viewpoints. Those who have felt left out, vulnerable, or victimized will need to take a risk and trust someone from "the other side." When individuals or groups who have been victimized begin to move toward reconciliation, they may experience anger, rage, fear, loneliness, and many other legitimate emotions. They must work through their desire for vengeance, but they must also consider the possibility that an expression of forgiveness is actually a cop-out. Persons who have experienced injustice should always question whether they could possibly be victimized or marginalized again. Before individuals let down their guard, they must be sure that they are ready; they must take serious precautions to avoid being made a fool. Yet without taking the risk of trusting, relationships can never be reconciled.

The one who must let go of power or acknowledge wrong-doing also has to take the risk of trusting. Professor Catherine Meeks writes about trust as it relates to race relations: "Most of the time a black person would not consider sharing with a white person what she is really thinking because no trust exists between them, and there is so much rage. Only the reality of trust in a relationship and its ability to bear up under the truth will allow rage to be shared. There are precious few places anywhere in the world where this can happen, and there are even fewer places where a black person would dare share his or her true feelings." Meeks confesses that this saddens her "because as long as we try to live in this atmosphere of unacknowledged feelings, we create an environment that allows us to be possessed by those feelings."[13] The willingness to receive a person's rage rather than run away or be defensive helps build trust. Daring to trust requires the ability to listen to the truth spoken by angry, pain-filled voices.

When I was a student at Howard University, one of my professors, Calvin Morris, noted that most of my encounters with African Americans had been "friendly" and noncon-frontational. He cared enough about me that he wanted to be sure that I was "real" and not just a white-bleeding-heart-do-gooder. So in class he proceeded to press all of my emotional buttons very forcefully. Morris was testing me to discover

whether I could deal with a strong and sometimes angry
black male. At first I was extremely intimidated. Then I got
mad. In fact, I began to feel hatred whenever I encountered
Calvin Morris. I finally went to him and requested forgiveness for how I was feeling. Morris knew I needed to address
some deep issues before I could move forward in the process
of working for reconciliation and growing in my ability to
trust (and be trusted).

Taking the risk of trusting others requires great courage. It
is a calculated risk and should be taken only after it has been
determined that one who has been hurt will not be rebrutal-
ized in the process. The person reaching out may have to
offer an olive branch of peace repeatedly before it is received.
Once it has been received, we must strap ourselves in and
prepare for an emotional roller-coaster ride. We may be
surprised by the depth of pain that has to be waded through,
our own as well as that of the other person. Relationships are
empowered when they take place between equals who need
each other, when they set people free, and when they include
all voices and viewpoints. The willingness to trust in the face
of severed relationships initiates the process of reconciliation
described in subsequent chapters.

Questions for Discussion

1. What are the required elements in relationships that are
equal? What needs to happen for us to recognize the interdependence of humanity?

2. How do efforts at reconciliation and liberation differ?
How are they similar? Can one ultimately be successful
without the other?

3. What does it mean truly to hear the voices and viewpoints of other people? How do we accomplish this goal?

4. What are some of the limitations we face when trying to understand another person's perspective on life?

5. In what ways are you multiculturally fluent? What suggestions do you have to further this process? Would the "Mutual Invitation" process for conducting meetings be feasible in your workplace or at your church?

6. What are the inherent risks in trusting? What are the positive possibilities? What are the trust factors currently inhibiting reconciliation?

7. What do you feel are the most important principles for reconciliation? Why?

Part III

A Costly Process

7

Taking Responsibility

For many years, Northern Ireland has suffered from a violent and deep division between the loyalists (Protestants) and the unionists (Roman Catholic). In an attempt to encourage a process of reconciliation, the "Peace People" began a bus service to the prisons. The bus service, which was available to both unionists and loyalists, provided a way for the wives of men who had been imprisoned during this conflict to visit their husbands. Often the wives of Protestant prisoners and the wives of Catholic prisoners rode together. The Peace People would then sponsor a project that called for wives from both sides to work together. Nobel Peace Prize winner Máiread Maguire comments:

> People said it won't work because the wives are from both sides of extremes and they just won't work together. But it did work and some of the deepest relationships came out of it. It's very important to try to find ways of bringing people from different groups together. Small is beautiful. We have to start small, wherever people are at.[1]

Whether we take small steps or large leaps, reconciliation is a process. We can state the problems with precision, proclaim the biblical mandate with eloquence, and commit ourselves to the principles, but unless we actually engage in a process, we will never experience reconciliation. I believe that the process of reconciliation must include the following steps: taking responsibility, seeking forgiveness, repairing the wrong, healing the soul, and creating a new way of relating. Other elements may be included, and the steps may occur in a different order or simultaneously (as is often the case). Yet I contend that reconciliation will rarely be achieved unless we strive to go through these steps in the process. This chapter will focus on what it means to take responsibility, while subsequent chapters will address the other steps.

Taking the First Step

Reconciliation is impossible until an individual (or a group of people) takes responsibility for the polarization that exists and takes action to create a better future. In August 1995 South African president Nelson Mandela hosted a lunch for the widows of former white presidents of South Africa and the widows of leaders of the black liberation movement. This initiative demonstrated the highly creative and very dramatic approaches to reconciliation that have been a hallmark of Mandela's presidency. Betsie Verwoerd chose not to attend the lunch that day. She was the ninety-four-year-old widow of former prime minister Hendrik Verwoerd, whose government had imprisoned Mandela for what eventually totaled twenty-seven years. In refusing the invitation to lunch, she casually mentioned that the president could stop by for tea sometime.

Two weeks after the luncheon, Nelson Mandela arrived in Orania, South Africa, for tea. Before the presidential entourage of over two hundred arrived, this small village, a "homeland" for 460 white-separatist extremists, had never seen so many blacks in one place. President Mandela and Mrs. Verwoerd spent forty-five minutes together. Then, with Betsie Verwoerd on his arm, Nelson Mandela escorted her out to make a statement. When the elderly woman struggled in her reading of the announcement, Mandela read part of it for her in Afrikaans. In the statement, Betsie Verwoerd, widow of a man who had considered Mandela the enemy, was now appealing for compassion: "I ask the president to consider the 'volkstaat' [homeland] with sympathy."[2] Nelson Mandela did not take revenge on his oppressors; nor did he wait for them to seek forgiveness. He took the responsibility for initiating a process of reunion.

If we believe that reconciliation is God's one-item agenda, then it is our responsibility to start the process. It does not matter on which side of the divide we find ourselves. It does not even matter whether we consider ourselves bystanders, outside of the problem, because none of us is exempt from the impact of an unhealthy society. All of us must take responsibility. The process of striving toward wholeness may begin when a number of people simultaneously start to work for reconciliation and a movement is born. Often one person like Nelson Mandela becomes the leader or the symbol of such an effort. It may also begin when two people, one from each side, take the bold step to meet each other. The manner in which the process is initiated is not as important as the fact that we choose to move toward peace and wholeness.

Unfortunately, some in the church have ignored the man-date to initiate the process of restoring relationships. Billy Graham has written that, in the past, he and other evangelical Christians "have turned a blind eye to racism or have been willing to stand aside while others take the lead in racial reconciliation, saying it was not our responsibility."[3] An equivalent statement could be made regarding issues related to gender, class, and other forms of prejudice. At the same time, as Calvin Morris reminds us, the initiative for reconcili-ation has often been one-sided:

> It fell to black American churches to call to the remem-
> brance of white and black Christians the biblical affirmation

that God made all the nations to dwell upon the face of
the earth. Despite their beleaguered circumstances and
virtual invisibility in white, Christian America, and
their long-standing obligation to provide black people "a shelter in a time of storms," black churches
have been in the forefront of the struggle for a racially
free and just America.[4]

Although the response to this call has not been overwhelming, many whites have responded. Perhaps the conversation about racial reconciliation these days owes its
origin to these African American churches that faithfully
reminded us that God created only one race, the human race.
Like black churches on the issue of race, women have often
either stood alone or been joined by a small number of men
in their efforts at gender equality. Interestingly, the leaders
for reconciliation tend more often to come from those groups
of people most directly affected by separation, while those in
a position of privilege may believe that reconciliation is
optional.

Because attempts at reconciliation may initially be singu-
lar efforts, they require courage and sometimes involve confrontation. One of the most repulsive situations I have ever
witnessed took place in a small group of Christian leaders,
all of whom were men. A respected leader proceeded to
illustrate one of his points by using a very vulgar, graphic,
and offensive description of women's sexuality. His "locker
room language," combined with his commodification of
women as sex objects, contrasted starkly with his public
statements of commitment to gender equality. Though I was
sickened by his comments, I am embarrassed to admit that I
said nothing because he was many years my senior. I chose
the easy way out rather than pay the cost of reconciliation.

The apostle Paul also faced a situation where a senior
leader of the church compromised the call of the gospel. In
this case it was the apostle Peter. In the second chapter of

Galatians (vv. 11-21), Paul stated that Peter had introduced ethnic segregation into the table fellowship at Antioch: Jews were eating with Jews, and Gentiles (Greeks, Africans, Romans, and so on) were eating with Gentiles. Peter's actions could have destroyed the Antioch church's ministry of reconciliation. Because of the evangelistic zeal of the Antioch congregation, this institutionalized prejudice would have adversely affected the entire region. After spending three years with Jesus, receiving a vision from God that Gentiles were "clean," and ministering directly to Cornelius, Peter was still held captive by his prejudice. So Paul courageously demonstrated what it means to take responsibility when individuals get in the way of God. Paul said, "I opposed him to his face" (2:11). He challenged Peter to repent from this compromise of the gospel. As Paul was obliged to rebuke Peter, a shared allegiance to Jesus Christ compels us to challenge the blind spots in the spiritual eyes of our brothers and sisters in the modern-day church, as well as in institutional structures, so that we can move forward with an agenda of reconciliation. Confrontation should be pursued in a spirit of love and only after much contemplation.

Discovering the Truth

Taking responsibility for initiating the process of reconnecting broken relationships is not enough. We must face our separation in all its ugliness. We must break through whatever forms of denial are impeding our progress. This effort requires that we make a commitment to discover the truth that exists on both sides. In many cases where division exists, there may be even more than two stories of alienation that must be heard in order to bring holistic healing to the relationship. We first must discover and name our own truth. We cannot attempt to remove the "speck" in the other's eye until we remove the "log" from our own eye (Matthew 7:3-5; Luke 6:41-42).

In chapter 5 I noted that self-examination is essential for
the reconciler. We may be unaccustomed to this process. In
fact, we may have a hard time identifying our own social
location. It may therefore be difficult to recognize our own
truth and our own responsibility. Experiential educator
Karen McKinney uses an exercise called "The Race" to help
individuals identify how the effects of injustice affect their
lives. Participants are asked to line up at a starting line for a
race. Before the race begins, each person must answer a series
of questions that will affect her or his placement at the
starting line. The exercise proceeds as follows:

*For each of the following questions that you can answer with a
yes, you can take a step forward:*

Were there fifty or more books in your house when you
   were growing up?
Was there a computer in your house?
Have you traveled to a foreign country?
Did both of your parents graduate from high school?
Did your parents have a savings account?
Did you have your own savings account as a child?
Did you see adults reading in your home on a regular
   basis?
Did your family take regular vacations to places other
   than the home of relatives?
Do your parents own their own home?
Do your parents have a second home or a summer
   home?
Did your family's recreation cost money, like skiing?
Did you have a car in high school?
Did you have a relative or friend who held a position of
   power in the community or company?
Did you attend a private school?
Did you attend camp in the summer?

Did most of the images you saw in school books look
   like you?
Did most of your teachers/administrators look like you?
Did the images you saw at church look like you?
Can you walk into hair shops and usually find someone
   there who can cut your kind of hair?
Can you shop at almost any supermarket and find the
   staple food of your culture on the shelves?
Can you make reservations and not wonder if people of
   your race are welcomed and well treated there?
Can you easily buy greeting cards and postcards with
   people like you on them?
Are you pretty sure you can buy a house anywhere you
   want and be welcomed by your neighbors?
If the police stop you, do you know that your race will
   not count against you?

*For each of these following questions that you can answer in the
affirmative you must take a step backward:*

Did you have a job in high school to help support your
   family?
Are you from a single-parent female-headed household?
Are you from a single-parent female-headed household
   where money was always an issue?
Have any of your family members had to sell or pawn
   something to pay for necessities?
Were you born in another country?
Is English a second language for you?
Is your everyday speech a black dialect?
Have you had a close relative or friend in prison?
Did you have a parent who was often unemployed (not
   by choice)?
Have you been told that you have a learning disability?
Were you routinely sent to the principal's office for be-
   havior issues?

Do your parents live from paycheck to paycheck?

Are family decisions made solely on the basis of money
  or lack thereof?

Are you female?

Did you qualify for free or reduced lunch in school?

Did you attend college completely dependent on financial aid?

Was one or both of your parents teens when you were
  born?

Was either of your parents partially or fully illiterate?

Are any of your family members on welfare?

Have you ever been in foster care?

Were police sirens a daily occurrence in your neighborhood?

Did you frequently hear the sound of bullets flying in
  your neighborhood?

Were abandoned houses within a half mile of where you
  lived when you grew up?

Have you ever been refused service because of your
  color?

Step back once if you are considered yellow, twice if you
  are considered brown, and three times if you are considered black.

Once all of the questions are answered, the participants are
asked to notice who is in front and who is in the back. This
exercise helps individuals name their social location. It also
visibly demonstrates the effects of injustice—a negative impact for some and a beneficial impact for others. Karen
McKinney then begins the race. As you would expect, those
at the front easily win. Some who are midway back try hard
to win but cannot overcome the odds. Those way behind the
starting line often just give up. "The Race" identifies the
existence of distinctions in society that result from injustice
and explores how they affect our lives and fuel the continu-
ation of such unjust division.[5]

While many are aware of the "negative" side of injustice, it is often less obvious that we can acquire privilege simply by benefiting from how society is arranged. An experiential exercise such as "The Race" can help us discover the truth about privilege. If we are in a privileged position in society because of our race, gender, socioeconomic status, or any other reason, a part of what it means to take responsibility is to acknowledge the fact that we are privileged. Even though we did not choose the social location of our birth, we did inherit a set of circumstances to which we must respond. Until we can speak the truth about our own situation, we cannot move forward in the process of relational bridge building. We certainly must speak the truth to ourselves and within our "own" groups. Often society's relational fragmentation has proceeded to the point where both sides have played a role in perpetuating division. Discovering the truth means identifying and verbalizing these past and present roles. Division in many parts of the world involves perpetrators, victims, and bystanders, as well as persons inheriting the deeds of their ancestors, on both sides of the divide. Sometimes in class, race, religious, or ethnic conflict multiple divisions exist. Eventually we must cross the boundaries and enter into dialogue with each other.

Feeling the Pain

Part of understanding the other's truth is feeling his or her pain. Taking responsibility means feeling the pain of isolation, tokenism, inferiority, fear, and rage. The powerful must feel the pain of the powerless. The victimizer must feel the pain of the vulnerable. Men must understand how women are affected by sexism and how sexism may shape their view of men. Whites need to understand the painful effects of racism on persons of color and grasp how this may affect their perception of whites. Persons who are middle-class or affluent need to discover the impact that poverty has on

people and learn how it can influence their view of those who
appear economically secure. Christians should learn how
Jews and Muslims experience an America in which they are
minority religions. To understand the suffering and rage of
the person who feels powerless in a relationship is an important ability. Samuel Hines describes his experience of this
phenomenon on a visit to South Africa in 1985: "From my
perspective, the most hopeful sign was the openness and
honesty of the Dutch Reformed Church people. It's the thing
I've been praying for and hoping for, and still it took me by
surprise. . . . people were able to sit down and listen to each
other's stories and hear each other cry."[6] Such occasions may
have helped facilitate a faster and more peaceful move toward freedom in South Africa.

True reconciliation also implies that the one who feels
victimized needs to understand the severe pain found deep
inside the oppressor that produces the desire to dominate.
What kind of trauma creates the Adolf Hitlers of this world?
During the civil rights movement, many high school and
college students came face to face with the internal ugliness
that created segregation. The story of one young woman,
part of a group who hoped to desegregate lunch counters by
participating in a sit-in, helps us comprehend the torment of
the oppressor. As the woman started to sit at the "whites
only" lunch counter, a plainclothes law enforcement officer
from another county told her to leave. She courageously
informed the officer that he had no authority in that county.
The officer then grabbed the woman, his fingernails piercing
her wrist, and shoved her against a wall. She described her
feelings as follows: "It was my very first direct encounter
with real violence. All the possibilities of what we were up
against had been drilled into us in our training and every
conceivable kind of situation had been simulated; but even
so, I was not prepared for the stark panic that moved through
me. This passed quickly and in its place I felt an intense and

angry violence—but something in me held." The young woman noted a shift in her feelings. She stated: "I looked him in the face until I felt his fear and sensed his own anguish. Then I thought, now quite calmly, how desperate a man must be to behave this way to a defenseless girl."[7]

In order to understand clearly the pain of the other, we must listen with compassion. We must suffer with those who are suffering. A compassionate ear values the story of others, listens without rendering judgment, and seeks to appreciate their perception of truth. Dietrich Bonhoeffer listened carefully and compassionately as he broke bread with Jews in Germany, served in poor and working-class parishes, and even traversed the city streets of Harlem in New York City. He learned to understand life "from the perspective of those who suffer."[8] He embraced a costly reconciliation because he intimately understood the pain of others and decided to take responsibility to end the suffering that was dividing Germany.

Articulating the Other's Experience

As we practice compassionate listening and begin to understand the truth and the pain of individuals on both sides, we must also learn how to communicate that pain to each other. We chip away at our polarization when we listen to the stories of those we consider different. Then we need to learn to retell those stories. We cannot assume that we comprehend another person's experience until we can articulate his or her truth and pain so clearly that the person affirms that we understand. Taking responsibility means that we take a bold step toward reconciliation by acknowledging our part in the separation, listening to the pain of others until we can feel it and articulate it, and committing to change the existing circumstances.

Questions for Discussion

1. How would you take the first step toward reconciliation with someone who was a victim? With an oppressor? With a bystander? With someone who was born into a situation of injustice but did not help create it?

2. Why do some Christians avoid taking responsibility for injustices in society?

3. Use the exercise "The Race" to identify your place in society. How do you feel about the results? What is your responsibility for reconciliation given your social location?

4. Do you believe that it is important to understand the pain of other persons in the process of creating harmony? Why or why not? What are some ways you can learn to feel another person's pain?

5. What does it mean to take responsibility for each of the following: sexism, classism, racism, homophobia, anti-Semitism, and other examples of injustice you want to include?

6. What are some other ways that we need to take responsibility not mentioned in this chapter?

7. What in this chapter was most helpful for you? Why?

8

No-Fault Reconciliation

Violette Nyirarukundo, at home with her family near the center of the capital city of Rwanda, was within earshot of the gunfire that began after the fatal downing of the plane carrying Rwanda's president in 1994. It was just a matter of time before the soldiers would be at her door. She instructed her family to hide beneath their beds. Shortly thereafter, bullets began shattering the windows of the house. From her hiding place Violette peeked out of the window closest to her and was shocked to see the face of a soldier with his gun pointing directly at her. Violette cried out that she would open the door and let him in. Three military men entered the house and beat Violette and her family because they were "the enemy." In an unanticipated, yet very courageous, move, Violette's teenage daughter asked the soldiers if they were going to kill her family. They responded that that was indeed their plan. Then the girl said, "We are Christians. May we pray before you kill us?" This brave act emboldened Violette, who grabbed a Bible and informed the intruders that this was the only weapon in the house. These fearless acts of witness to their faith in Jesus Christ unsettled the soldiers. After taking their money, the military men decided to leave, saying, "We do not want the blood of Christians on our hands. Others will come after us and kill you." Several other groups of angry soldiers did come by the Nyirarukundo home. They saw that the windows were broken, assumed that the inhabitants had already been killed, and continued to the next residence.

As I sat in a restaurant listening to Violette recount this incident, I was deeply moved by the lack of bitterness in her voice. She even added, with a touch of humor, that she and her family were disappointed when the soldiers did not kill them. For in that moment, they had made their peace and were ready to go to heaven. Now they had to remain on this earth. Violette Nyirarukundo currently works for reconciliation among the Rwandan people. During our conversation, she revealed the secret of her ability to do this: she had unconditionally forgiven the soldiers.[1] Violette could unconditionally forgive the soldiers who had wanted to kill her and her family because she had experienced the forgiveness of the one who, while hanging on the cross, said, "Father, forgive them; for they do not know what they are doing" (Luke 23:34). Violette Nyirarukundo demonstrated the forgiveness needed for the process of reconciliation to move forward.

Forgiveness repairs the relational damage that results from separation. It produces a change in the heart and an attitude adjustment for both the one offering it and the one receiving it. It breathes life into our relationships with God and each other. Forgiveness creates what sociologist C. Eric Lincoln calls "no-fault reconciliation—the recognition that we are all of a kind, with the same vulnerabilities, the same possibilities, and the same needs for God and each other."[2] This "no-fault reconciliation" that springs from the act of forgiveness helps us move away from a need to blame.

Forgiveness Is Freedom

The decision to forgive or seek forgiveness is ours. With God it is always reciprocal. We ask God to be forgiven and we are—fully and unconditionally—but this may not happen in our human relationships. Forgiveness, though, does not hinge upon whether we gain the response we seek. Forgiveness is a healing act, releasing the pain that comes from anger or fear. Forgiveness opens the door for reconciliation. When reciprocated, it leads us to come together in a relationship. Without forgiveness there is no reconciliation. The act of forgiving is a freeing experience: it allows us to refocus our anger on injustice rather than on the perpetrator(s) of injustice. It helps us release our desire for retribution. Even though revenge may give us a momentary feeling of justice, it simply increases the separation we experience in the human family. God will deal with those who are unrepentant (Deuteronomy 32:35; Romans 12:19).

Forgiveness enables us to recognize the humanity in the other person. We may even begin to comprehend what motivated their choices (even their wrong choices). Forgiveness is liberating.[3] Forgiveness grants us freedom from our own personal history or one we have inherited through society. It is often our inability to let go of pain from the past that inhibits our ability to engage in efforts leading toward reconciliation in the present. When we listen to the pain of those whom we find hard to forgive, we are better able to extend forgiveness. Deliverance from the prison of past wrongs can be found through offering and receiving forgiveness.

The Evidence of Repentance

Sometimes forgiveness is blocked by a lack of trust. Reconciliation cannot be achieved without trust. Repairing the wrong that was committed is a way to restore trust. When marriage vows are violated by adultery, one can be successfully reunited with his or her spouse only if trust can be restored. This often requires some sort of "proof" that the erring spouse has truly changed. I believe this need for evidence is an important ingredient in reconciliation, particularly when one party has been victimized. Without some form of confirmation that there has been a change, there may be no interest in reuniting. People can offer moving statements or dramatic presentations that acknowledge wrongdoing and a desire for reconciliation, but without action they are like "a noisy gong or a clanging cymbal" (1 Corinthians 13:1). Forgiveness without the evidence of repentance can produce a cheap reconciliation.

Some years ago a group of United States veterans from the Vietnam War initiated the Veterans Vietnam Restoration Project. They used a three-step process. First, they went to Vietnam and acknowledged that the war had caused injury. In other words, they took responsibility for the effects of their actions. Then they offered "active compensation in the very places where they had fought by restoring, with their own hands, what they had earlier destroyed." These veterans built health-care facilities in the villages and cities they had attacked and bombed. Finally, they asked "forgiveness of their former enemies and their descendants."[4] Forgiveness was requested only after they had concretely demonstrated their repentance by repairing the wrongs that were committed.

Although the process of reconciliation begins as we take responsibility for understanding and addressing the discord in society, we also need to repair the wrong done in order to restore relationships to wholeness. When we truly take responsibility for disunity, we engage in efforts to remove the barriers that exist and restore the original unity intended for the human family. Forgiveness and reparations are complementary actions. Christian theology is based on the importance of forgiving and repairing wrong. Jesus was physically nailed to a cross as a concrete demonstration that we are forgiven of our sins and that our relationship with God, which had been severed by sin, has been restored. The cross enables us to trust that our relationship with God has been reconciled. The cross portrays forgiveness and reparation as two important aspects of reconciliation. Costly reconciliation calls us not only to forgive but to repair wrongs committed, whether or not we were the offending party.

Reestablishing Truth

Post-apartheid South Africa is experimenting with what it means to juxtapose forgiveness with justice in the process of reconciliation. Archbishop Desmond Tutu is presiding over the South African Truth and Reconciliation Commission. All sides have been invited to come and tell the truth about their pain or the crimes they committed. A number of key leaders from both sides of the apartheid system have come forward and acknowledged abuses. Many people who experienced a violation of their human rights during the apartheid system, and did not experience justice, are coming forward to tell their stories. Charles Villa-Vicencio writes that some who come "simply want to know the truth, so that they can put the past behind them. More than one person has insisted that they simply need to know *who* killed their husband, maimed their child, or destroyed their lives in order to be able to face the challenge of forgiveness."[5] Jesus said that if you "know the truth . . . the truth will make you free" (John 8:32). One of the first things that must be repaired if trust is to be restored is truth. Once again, using marital reconciliation after an affair as an example, in order for the offended spouse to take the risk to trust again, the truth must be reestablished.

Knowing the truth is also important for relationships in a society. If our beliefs about other people (or groups of people) are based on misinformation or stereotypes or lies, then these must be removed and replaced by the truth before reconciliation can occur. In American society, the lie that "maleness" or "whiteness" is the norm is often subtly endorsed. Sometimes we identify people by race or gender when they do not fit the prescribed norm, even though that fact may have no relevance in our conversation. For instance, we might say: "My co-worker, an Asian, played golf with me today" or "My accountant, a woman, helped me prepare my taxes." I once heard a white preacher speaking to a predominantly African American congregation tell a story about a "little black girl." Her blackness was not germane to the story. Most members of the congregation probably would have imagined her as black. Identifying an individual by her or his race or gender, when it is irrelevant, may reveal a subtle belief that the person is different from "the norm." We must reestablish the truth that humanity is the norm. No one created in the image of God is outside of God's norm. The truth of our shared humanity is essential for reconciliation.

For trust to be restored, the truth of history must also be repaired. When I read Ronald Takaki's book, *A Different Mirror: A History of Multicultural America*,[6] I was surprised at how much I did not know about the origins of the United States and the degree to which I had been misinformed about certain subjects. It also became clear that those in power, the victors, write history. It is equally clear that women, the poor, people of color, indigenous people, and others marginalized in their setting *must* contribute to the task of writing history. If we are ignorant of significant portions of history, we cannot understand what created the division and the injustice we experience today. Until we know the historical reasons for our problems today, we will be limited in our ability to suggest solutions. It is only when all histories exist side by side that we can, in dialogue, gain a truer understanding of our shared life together on this planet. This multicultural fluency improves the potential for reconciliation.

As I suggested in chapter 3, our understanding of Jesus Christ has been at the center of this struggle to reclaim truth. The Afro-Asiatic Galilean Jew from Nazareth named Jesus was changed into a historical person with roots in Europe. The search for a more historically accurate image of Jesus is important to reconciliation because of the damage done by the lie of a white Jesus. This fabrication has also limited, and often inhibited, the possibility of the image of a universal Christ taking on flesh in various cultural settings.[7] In my book *Coming Together* I brought together six examples of cultural understandings of Jesus Christ that have emerged in recent years as biblical interpretation has become more inclusive. The six images are: the Gold-Crowned Jesus, the Galilean *Jíbaro* Jesus, Jesus the One Crowned with Thorns, Jesus the Great Healer, the Jim-Crowed Jesus, and Jesus the Truth Teller.[8] When cultural interpretations of Christ are studied in concert with a more accurate understanding of the historical Jesus of Nazareth portrayed in the Gospels, the truth of Jesus Christ can be communicated more fully.

The story of Francisco Penning's aunt from chapter 3 illustrates this point. She prayed exclusively to Mary because she could not relate to a royal white Jesus Christ. Francisco believes that if his aunt were alive today, and were given the truth, "she would pray to the Galilean *Jíbaro* [peasant] Jesus." He adds: "Today I pray to Him with joy in my heart knowing that He hears me and can relate to what I have been through. The challenge for me is to take the gospel of a *Jíbaro* Jesus to those in my homeland who do not know him. My aunt's tears were not in vain. I believe God answered her many prayers through the Virgin Mary. Today those tears reminded me not of the effects of a white Jesus who is indifferent to my cries, but of a *Jíbaro* Jesus who listens."[9]

In order to reclaim truth, we need to use our best thinking to discover the truth that helps produce a no-fault reconciliation.[10] We have assigned our brightest minds to a wide range of studies but have failed to utilize much of this brain power for creating a reconciled world. We in the church (and in society) need to encourage our most creative thinkers to seek remedies for the various forms of injustice and division that exist. We need to support innovative attempts to develop ways for diverse peoples to live together as members of the household of God and as citizens of planet Earth. When our best thinking is devoted to repairing the broken bridges that cross the cavern of human diversity, we are closer to achieving God's one-item agenda.

Acts of Justice

The purpose of repairing wrongs goes beyond the need to restore trust and truth. Reparations should reconstruct the equality of social and economic relationships, as well as create a just balance of power within society (and the church). Naim Ateek, a Palestinian pastor and theologian, states: "Begin with justice, and then you will see me running for reconciliation. . . . You have to begin by confessing that injustice has been done and beginning with a gesture of justice."[11] As a Palestinian, he believes that such a "gesture of justice" would be manifested in the creation of a Palestinian state. I believe that regardless of the setting, acts of justice need to include both reparation of physical damage through community and economic development and reparation of systemic damage through socially just legislation. Declaring that we are all equal without repairing the wrongs of the past is cheap reconciliation.

I have observed three approaches to repairing societal wrongs. In the first approach, those in power offer to repair the wrong they or their predecessors have caused. After the issuing of the Emancipation Proclamation, the government of the United States proclaimed that formerly enslaved Africans would each be given forty acres and a mule as repayment for several generations of free labor. While this was far from adequate compensation, its implementation would have greatly strengthened the overall economic condition of African Americans. Affirmative action was another attempt by those in power to help women, people of color, and individuals who were poor gain access to the system. Unfortunately, efforts organized by governments and ruling parties rarely include a change in the balance of power. In fact, some of the economic improvements offered are actually attempts at either appeasement or assimilation. Some of the efforts encouraging racial integration in the United States have been merely methods for absorbing people of color into mainstream white society. As social justice activist Jim Wallis states: "What is most wrong with integration is simply this: It always has taken place and now proceeds on white terms. . . . Integration begs the question—integration into what?"[12]

A second approach used for creating a more just society is the development of partnerships. This shared approach can be initiated by either group. One way that such partnerships occur is when urban and suburban congregations work together. A suburban congregation can provide economic and volunteer support for community development projects run by a congregation in an urban neighborhood. The urban congregation can help repair damage in the suburban community that has resulted from separation. This could include workshops on the effects of racism, materialism, and classism. As a result of surviving with limited resources, many urban congregations have also developed a vibrant spirituality. This may serve to renew the faith of members in suburban congregations. These efforts are strengthened when planning and implementation are done jointly. A congregation that left the city for the suburbs because of a change in the racial or economic composition of its neighborhood might develop a creative plan for reentry. The Veterans Vietnam Restoration Project offers an intriguing model. The suburban congregation could return to the same city neighborhood it left and work with a congregation or agency there to develop a concrete act of restitution that might lead to reconciliation. This could include building a house, opening a medical clinic, or whatever residents of that community identify as a need.[13]

Another example of this second approach is seen when charitable foundations partner with community-based non-profits to restore social and economic health. Such associations must empower community organizations, and participating foundations must avoid excessive control of program development. Interestingly, although the gospel calls us to reconcile the rich and poor, very few Christian charitable foundations are committed to such an agenda. This makes it difficult for Christian organizations that work for reconciliation and social justice to fund their ministries. The Wallestad Foundation in Minneapolis, Minnesota, represents an exception. The foundation was begun by the late Victor C. Wallestad, a Christian philanthropist and president of Fluoroware, Inc., a worldwide manufacturer of plastic products with headquarters in Chaska, Minnesota. Wallestad's lawyer, Jay Bennett, encouraged him to organize his giving to Christian missions and evangelism by establishing a foundation. This Wallestad did, naming Bennett its president.

Under Bennett's direction, the foundation has expanded its work to include Christian agencies addressing economic and community development, reconciliation, and other concerns facing the cities of Minneapolis and St. Paul. Rather than limiting its role to grant making, the Wallestad Foundation prefers to establish partnerships that promote positive community change through living out the call of the gospel. This creative shift occurred because Jay Bennett took the initiative to discover what was happening in the city. The foundation's giving priorities are influenced by what Bennett learns from community leaders, and thus its economic investments actually empower organizations serving in the urban community.

I have observed a third approach when the powerless

themselves repair identified wrongs. Such efforts emerge when those in power show no interest in repairing societal wrongs. In fact, with this approach, the powerless no longer qualify for that label because, as they control their own destinies, they become empowered. Winona LaDuke, an activist for the rights of indigenous people throughout the world, launched the White Earth Land Recovery Project (WELRP) in Minnesota to buy back the original lands of the Anishinaabeg nation after "a decade of land rights organizing, and the loss of three federal law suits to recover land."[14] When she began the project with the proceeds of her 1988 Reebok Human Rights Award, over 90 percent of the original 837,000 acres reserved for the Anishinaabeg by a treaty with the U.S. government in 1867 were in the hands of non-Indian people. Since those in power chose not to participate in amending this wrong, the WELRP began the process of reparation on its own. To date over 1,000 acres have been purchased. The goal is to buy back another 30,000 acres in the next fifteen years. The acquisition of land is only part of a strategy that includes cultural, economic, and spiritual repair. WELRP is developing a sustainable economic base and launching educational efforts aimed at maintaining the Anishinaabeg culture and language. Not only are the White Earth Land Recovery Project and similar efforts empowering to those who participate, but they also may be able to repair economic, social, and spiritual harm.

The three approaches described above produce different results. When reparations come from the impetus of those in power, they frequently fall short of true reconciliation because the voices of those who have been hurt by injustice are rarely included. Often these efforts are designed so that they serve the interests of those in control; they fail to empower the recipients and leave unchanged the structure of power relationships. The partnership approach, if carried out in a manner that exemplifies true equality, holds the greatest

potential for genuine reconciliation. The third approach reminds us that the powerful may not want to reconcile. If we
receive a negative response from the party with whom we
are seeking to engage in the process of repairing societal
wrongs, we need not curtail our efforts. Winona LaDuke
obviously understands that her Anishinaabeg people on the
White Earth reservation must not be held captive by the
self-interests of others. Though one-sided reparation is not
the ideal, it is often the only viable alternative available. The
process of reconciliation must move forward.

A Symbolic Gesture

Acts of reparation take on different forms depending on
the root cause of or history surrounding the polarization.
Concrete acts like the Veterans Vietnam Restoration Project
and the White Earth Land Recovery Project are important
and necessary. Symbolic actions can serve the important role
of catalyst for reconciliation because they "operate at a
deeper level where the wrestling is with the loyalties, ban-
ners, and spells that rule a way of life and its institutions."[15]
Since reconciliation also requires that our hearts and minds
be repaired, we should never underestimate the power of
symbolic gestures.

In December 1981 I was living in Times Square with the
Covenant Community, a group of Christians who committed
themselves to prayer, community, simplicity, and service.[16]
During the Christmas season that year, a number of us decided to go Christmas caroling in our neighborhood. I must
admit that I had never experienced Christmas caroling like
this. Our first stop was the Port Authority bus station. As we
sang, we were joined by people who were living on the
streets or who were victims of the area's thriving sex indus-
try. Many presumably continued their life on the streets, but
perhaps we planted a small seed of hope that eventually
blossomed into a better life. Our next stop was an adult

bookstore. No one joined us as we sang, "round yon virgin mother and child." The men who entered and left the sex shop either expressed anger or dropped their heads in shame and embarrassment. Many of them probably returned to pornographic bookstores in subsequent days, but perhaps one remembered his wife and children at home and decided to honor his vow of faithfulness.

Though I have no idea what happened to the people who heard us sing, I want to believe that for someone in Times Square, the evening was transformed into a silent night and a holy night. Christmas caroling in the bright lights of Times Square was a symbolic gesture that reminded us all of that night when the sky was filled with the bright lights of a multitude of angels singing, "Glory to God in the highest heaven, and on earth peace among those whom he favors!" (Luke 2:14). By electing to minister in Times Square that night, we announced that the breach between rich and poor, perpetrator and victim, and God and humanity had been repaired because the reconciler par excellence "became flesh and lived among us" (John 1:14). No-fault reconciliation is at the core of our faith as Christians. The same Jesus who lived among us and modeled reconciliation died a redemptive death that brought forgiveness and restored our relationship with God. The cross reminds us that we must forgive and request forgiveness. It also reminds us that we must restore trust, reestablish truth, and, with justice, repair the social and economic rupture in society.

Questions for Discussion

1. In your own words, how would you define *no-fault reconciliation?* Why is this an important concept?

2. What does it mean to forgive someone? What does it mean to request forgiveness from someone? Describe the role of forgiveness in bridging the divide that currently exists

between those of different gender, economic class, race, cultures, and denominations. Are there other areas of division you would like to add?

3. Define *repentance*. When is it important for there to be evidence of repentance? Cite some examples. In what ways do forgiveness and repairing the wrong intersect? What is the role of the cross in reconciliation?

4. What is involved in reestablishing truth in relationships? Can trust ever fully be restored? Why or why not?

5. Why is it important to know the truth about Jesus? What happens when truth is hidden or compromised? How can we create opportunities for more of our best thinkers to focus their energies on resolving the costly problems of human division facing our world?

6. Identify the three approaches to reparations that the author discussed. Compare and contrast them. Share examples that you have observed. Are there any other approaches that you are aware of? If so, name them. What is your opinion about the value of symbolic actions?

7. What in this chapter provided you with a better understanding of the process of reconciliation? Why?

9

Resting in the Womb of God

In December 1994 I visited the Hawaiian Islands for the first time. What I experienced during those few days far surpassed my expectations. It would have been impossible for me to predict, and it is still difficult to comprehend fully, the effect that visiting the islands had on my soul. Their majestic natural beauty ministered to me in very deep and mysterious ways. Feeling the heat of the bright and welcoming sun stimulated and enlivened my body. Walking in the cool sand focused and reinvigorated my mind. Listening to the soothing sound of the waves rejuvenated my tired soul. The restorative power I enjoyed while on these peaceful, gentle islands was exhilarating. This sense of mystical tranquility was particularly intense as I walked along the enchantingly beautiful Waimanalo Beach on Oahu. (This beach is affectionately called "the healing beach" by friends who live on the island.) With mountains on one side and ocean on the other, with blue sky over my head and sand under my feet, I felt extremely secure and unconditionally loved. While the waves caressed my weary spirit, the stresses of life were released, and I relished a profound sense of restfulness. I delighted in the awareness that I belonged. I recognized a feeling of homecoming. I wanted to stay forever. Upon returning to the mainland, I could only say that I had been *resting in the womb of God.*

The process of reconciliation requires that we experience a deep healing of the soul, both as individuals and as a society. Taking responsibility, forgiving, and repairing wrongs are important ingredients in this healing process. Yet there may be a deeper pain that endures. This hurt cannot be completely eased until we discover a way to rest in the womb of God. Even though we are reconciled with God and our brothers and sisters, we may still need to find peace within ourselves. Our own souls need healing. Since most of us cannot travel to Hawaii for this cure (and of course, even in "paradise" there are problems and anxiety), we must seek a therapy for our souls that can be experienced right where we live. In this chapter I take a closer look at the inner pain that persists and the healing that is available from God. At times this chapter may seem a bit heavy, and perhaps troubling, to read. Stay with me, because healing is an essential part of the process of reconciliation.

The Crisis of Identity

I believe that at the root of our need for deep personal and societal healing is a crisis of identity. Many of the wars throughout history and much of the domestic strife today were born from a need to assert one's individual or group identity at the expense of others. Also much of the division found in society is based on efforts to define and distinguish ourselves, whether by religion, race, ethnicity, or gender. Máiread Maguire reminds us that in her country of Northern Ireland, "People will kill to defend their identity, their Britishness or Irishness."[1] The act of exalting one's identity over another's by embracing a false sense of superiority cuts off any meaningful interaction with other members in the human family. It greatly limits one's ability to experience communion with God as well, because we are ignoring

God's intent in creation. I believe a crisis of identity can cause a virus in our souls.

Family psychotherapist Gary Steele believes that his racial prejudice was fueled by an overwhelming sense of despair and a lack of self-esteem. His identity crisis was exacerbated by a heavy sense of grief and loss because he had experienced a number of violent and traumatic events. Gary was involved in many physical altercations and also had the misfortune of seeing people die. His response was to relieve his lingering depression and aching self-esteem with violence and alcohol. His violence, both verbal and physical, was at times directed toward Native Americans. Gary believes that stories from Native America caused him to explode violently because they had "a familiar sound." The loss of tribal lands somehow reminded him of his own loss and hurt. He reflects, "Racism provided an easy relief for my pain as I wanted to drown out the painful reminder of my own losses." Even after Gary became a Christian and later graduated from seminary, he still struggled with racism. Although he took responsibility for his attitudes and actions and asked forgiveness for his sins, his racism persisted. He had not resolved the underlying issues that were fueling his own personal crisis of identity.[2]

Although bigotry can be generated by unhealed trauma and low self-esteem, for some the sting of prejudice *is* the source of unresolved hurt. Social caste systems, which create hierarchies based on biological attributes, physical characteristics, social environment, economic status, and so on, can give birth to perceptions of inferiority and a crisis of identity. The daily assault of racism, sexism, classism, and other forms of bigotry wounds the inner psyche. Self-esteem is battered and souls are scarred by attacks that imply unworthiness. Such oppression from without can lead to a depression within. One may not even be aware of how severely he or she has been harmed. When a person has experienced over time the indignities resulting from bigotry, she or he may become traumatized. The rage discussed in chapter 2 could be a response to the trauma and stress that results from the experience of oppression. Bigotry is a violation of God's design for humanity. When this design is disregarded and oppression takes its place, individuals can collapse psychologically. If we feel powerless to change or dismantle forms of injustice, we may become overwhelmed. So we must take seriously the cries originating deep within our souls which call for healing from the scars of injustice.

The Pain That Is Inherited

The alienation felt internally may be inherited from our family, cultural, or religious history. We know that the children of abuse victims and alcoholics are at high risk for experiencing the lingering effects of such trauma. In the same way, oppression may have an impact on subsequent generations. Do the descendants of slaves carry cultural wounds passed on from those who originally experienced such dehumanization? Do women's psyches bear the scars of a history of exclusion? Have Native Americans suffered any consequences from a history of forced assimilation and attempted genocide? Does poverty leave any emotional marks on the grandchildren of its victims? I expect that, as a society, we do pass on some of this dysfunction from generation to generation, through our culture, family, and religion. In our efforts to heal the enduring pain of division, we must also ponder these possible effects of a history of oppression.

What happens when someone who has been oppressed gains power but has never experienced any healing from the effects of his or her maltreatment? We have learned in our society that many who perpetrate abuse were once victims themselves. Their unhealed wounds become the engine that drives their own violence. So we could expect that some of the injustice in society stems from the formerly oppressed

who have not been healed. Perhaps a fear of revictimiza-
tion is a part of this scenario. The European men who
conquered the Americas were, in many cases, fleeing persecution in their own countries of origin. They may have
internalized their previous experience of oppression and
feared the possibility of being revictimized. Psychotherapist
Nicholas Cooper-Lewter notes that "the issue was not
simply white or black, or male or female, or rich or poor or
whatever dualistic opposites. The issue was who will be the
master and who will be the slave. Ingrained in oppression of
African Americans was the pain European immigrants
brought from their own homelands. Seeing an opportunity
to get out from under abuse, they built a culture that relied
on oppression for domination."[3]

Patterns of domination trap people in dehumanizing
structures. When there are no other models, previously oppressed people who achieve liberation may simply adapt the
structures of power that were used against them. The cycle
of oppression begins again. Soon another group of people
will need to be set free because they are being mistreated by
those who were previously abused. True freedom requires
that we experience healing from the desire to have power
over the destinies of other people. In order to break the cycle
that leads to a new generation of oppressors, people who are
liberated must experience a deep healing in their souls before
they are empowered.[4]

There also may be serious wounds among the descendants
of those who misused power to dominate others. Do men
feel the residual effects of their forefathers' many centuries
of treating women as second-class citizens? Do descendants of the economic elite experience any repercussions
as a result of the deeds of their ancestors? Do the great-great-
grandchildren of slave owners bear the psychological bruises
of their foreparents' actions? Perhaps the denial, arrogance,
and fear described in chapters 1 and 2 are examples of the

effects of an inheritance of unhealed pain. A few years ago, while visiting New York City, I went to Harlem to buy a hat for a coworker. He had given me general directions to a marketplace near the Apollo Theater where he believed that this type of hat could be purchased. I had been to Harlem numerous times, having served as an associate minister in a church in northern Harlem. As a white person in this African American cultural mecca, I had been comfortable. Though I had never visited this section of Harlem before, I felt confident that I would have no problems. I emerged from the subway station onto the street on a beautiful summer day. The streets were full of people selling items that included shirts with Malcolm X's face and many objects that proudly displayed the colors of Africa. As soon as I stepped onto the street and began to search for the hat I planned to purchase, I was seized by an intense and emotionally raw sense of fear. I did not see a beautiful day in an exciting urban marketplace. What I saw was the anger displayed on the T-shirt with Malcolm X's face that read, "By any means necessary." What I saw were hundreds of black people, and I was the only white person in sight. And what I did not see was the hat I had intended to purchase.

For some reason, all of the "tapes" in my mind that contained negative stereotypes about African Americans were triggered. I quickly tried to rein in these out-of-control emotions as I searched the marketplace for the hat. I told myself that I had no reason to fear. This was a safe section of Harlem. No one was acting in a threatening manner. People were just going about their business. I even analyzed my emotions as I walked the streets of Harlem: my imagination had been seized by deeply ingrained stereotypes that I had somehow absorbed from U.S. culture, I told myself. The people I saw in the marketplace that day did not want to hurt me simply because I was white. Yet despite my best arguments, I was unable to free myself from what had become a nearly overwhelming sense of fear. Since I could neither calm my internal emotional state nor find the hat I was so desperately searching for, I went to the only person that I could identify as safe—a police officer. Interestingly, the officer was also an African American, but his blue uniform seemed to counteract his black skin in my mind. I asked him if he knew where I could find this hat, but he did not, so I left Harlem, finally able to quiet my emotions.

As I left, I was disturbed by the fact that my knowledge and beliefs had not been able to prevent my emotional response to the situation. I believed in reconciliation. I did not accept as valid any of the stereotypes that had so permeated my mind in Harlem. What I came to understand was that I needed to be healed from what I had inherited through the legacy of being born white in American society. Somewhere, buried within my inner being, I had been scarred by these inherited beliefs and irrational fears. For some reason, on that beautiful day in Harlem, the wound emerged from its hiding place.

I wonder what other effects our society feels as a result of historical injustices passed on through the culture. Perhaps some of the serious issues we face in our world stem from unhealed pain or past oppression. Former U.S. president Thomas Jefferson, a slave owner who loved to intellectualize about the negative effects of slavery, did believe that the behavior of slave owners could be passed on to the next generation. He warned:

> The whole commerce between master and slave is a perpetual exercise of the most boisterous passions, the most unremitting despotism on the one part, and degrading submissions on the other. Our children see this, and learn to imitate it; for man is an imitative animal. . . . If a parent could find no motive either in his philanthropy or his self-love, for restraining the intemperance of passion toward his slave, it should

always be a sufficient one that his child is present. But generally it is not sufficient. The parent storms, the child looks on, catches the lineaments of wrath, puts on the same airs in the circle of smaller slaves, gives a loose to his worst of passions, and thus nursed, educated, and daily exercised in tyranny, cannot but be stamped by it with odious peculiarities. The man must be a prodigy who can retain his manner and morals undepraved by such circumstances.[5]

Given Jefferson's contention, what happened after the Emancipation Proclamation ended legalized slavery? When there were no longer slaves to beat or rape, was this learned behavior unleashed in other ways in society?[6] If our culture does pass on some of the psychological and spiritual sicknesses of society to subsequent generations, then a very deep healing will be needed if reconciliation is to be accomplished.

What Does Health Look Like?

I believe that there is hope for reconciliation and healing in our society. The bad news of our crisis of identity and inherited pain can be overcome by the good news of a God who truly loves us and wants us to be whole. The message of reconciliation with God is that through Jesus Christ we can become a "new creation" (2 Corinthians 5:17), at peace with God. The old can pass away and everything can become new. In order to pursue wholeness, we must recognize what health looks like. I like pastoral counselor Gene Knudsen Hoffman's summary of some characteristics that are evident when we are healthy, that is, reconciled to God, others, and ourselves:

Healthy people are not destructive. They do not wound nor annihilate one another with guns or bombs. Healthy people are able to share; they are concerned for the well-being of others. They are grateful for life, and have compassion for others—even their enemies. Healthy people have hope, and a purpose in life. They are faithful to the truth they perceive until another is revealed. They don't harbor blame, resentment, or antipathy. This doesn't mean they don't feel these emotions; undoubtedly they do, but they don't hold on to or act upon them. Healthy people don't suffer from a denial of harm they have done, or of errors in judgement they have made. In short, they take responsibility for their part of any problem.

Healthy people are willing to work through conflict toward solutions, trusting that these solutions might be different from any they could have imagined. They are open and flexible, with the faith that a way will open to resolution. Healthy people see their own need for forgiveness, so they are ready to forgive others. They nurture gifts and self-strengthening propensities in others, and treat themselves and others with respect. They do not permit themselves or others to be abused. Healthy people make the same mistakes as non-healthy people do, but they are more aware of them and care for their boundaries and limits. Healthy people live lives of service to others.[7]

The health of a society and the health of individuals are intertwined and cannot be realized apart from each other. A healthy society safeguards the health of its citizens and also helps create a new generation of healthy individuals. The rest of this chapter offers a framework for moving closer to the reality of healthy people and communities.

A Therapy for the Soul

The prophet Jeremiah cried out rhetorically: "Is there no balm in Gilead? Is there no physician there? Why then has the health of my poor people not been restored?" (Jeremiah 8:22). I believe that there is a source of healing, a balm in Gilead. God can heal our souls. Although I am not a psychologist, I am aware that some of the effects of the trauma of bigotry will require professional attention. I do not underestimate the importance of psychotherapy. Yet I believe that God can relieve the pain that comes from bruised self-esteem and a legacy of oppression. Faith in God is *the* essential ingredient in our hope for a deep inner healing. As stated in chapter 4, reconciliation begins when we make peace with God. The Almighty reaches out and invites us into a relationship. When we accept this invitation, we discover peace. We cannot hope to make relations right with others if we are not in a right relationship with God.

Yet we need more than just a right relationship with God; we need a union where we can rest in the womb of God. We need to establish a therapeutic relationship with God. We need to be engaged in what Nicholas Cooper-Lewter calls "soul therapy."[8] When we were in the womb of our mother we felt safe, secure, and stable. We were sheltered from the stress that one encounters in the world. The womb was our home, and we knew we belonged. The rhythmic movement of this close, warm environment created a sense of restfulness. In my womblike experience at Waimanalo Beach in Hawaii, the beauty of the surroundings directed my attention to the goodness of God. Cooper-Lewter believes that many ancient cultures used an understanding of the prenatal experience in the womb as a source of healing. He states that these "experiences of safety, security, [and] stability served as ideals for future strategies for evaluating fears faced and anxieties overcome. . . . Soul therapy cultivated attitudes about harmonious partnerships with Creator and creation, and how information should be organized for health [and] wholeness in ways to prevent, counter-act, cope [with] and overcome insults to who people were."[9] Making peace with God can initiate such a process of inward healing and transformation.

The image of the womb raises the issue of identity. For many of us, our self-understanding is linked to the experience of our birth. The parameters of our humanity are defined by our genealogical, cultural, racial, ethnic, gender, or class origins. The words of the prophet Isaiah point us in a different direction:

> Listen to me, O house of Jacob,
> all the remnant of the house of Israel,
> who have been borne by me from your birth,
> carried from the womb;
> even to your old age I am he,
> even when you turn gray I will carry you.
> I have made, and I will bear;
> I will carry and will save.
> —Isaiah 46:3-4

Through the voice of the prophet, God reminded the Hebrew people that, even in captivity, the source of their identity must be their relationship with God. Sociologist C. Eric Lincoln notes that this has been the secret of faith in African American communities: "*Anybody who was a child of God could never be nobody,* and on that slender filament of faith the reconstruction of the African American sense of self would ultimately depend."[10] To put it more colloquially, knowing *whose* we are helps us know *who* we are. Learning to see ourselves as God sees us enables us to rest in the knowledge that we are children of God and brothers and sisters to all of humanity.

The following story illustrates the power of a God-centered identity. One day two young girls encountered each other. One girl was well-dressed and came from a rich home. The other girl was clothed in rags. The wealthy girl spoke first, saying, "Do you see that nice house up on that hill? That is my father's house. Do you see those cows grazing in the field? Those are my father's cows. Do you see those horses drinking from the lake? Those are my father's horses." In response to the first girl's boasting, the second girl replied: "Do you see the hill that your father's house sits on? That is my father's hill. Do you see the field that your father's cows are grazing in? That is my father's field. Do you see the lake that your father's horses are drinking from? That is my father's lake." The rich girl incredulously exclaimed, "If this is true, then why are you dressed so raggedy?" The second girl responded, "You are coming from your father's house while I am on my way to my father's house."[11] The second girl was secure in the understanding that her source of identity did not come from what could be seen but from what was unseen. Her self-esteem was rooted in her connection with God. A God-centered identity frees us from others' expectations or pronouncements. We can feel secure in our self. We can even experience restfulness because God will carry our sense of identity from birth to old age. We never have to feel insecure when we are in the womb of God.

In addition to grounding our identity, the idea of entering the womb of God takes us to a time before our personal history. It suggests that we do not have to be defined or held captive by our mistakes or the dysfunction of our family of origin. We can truly become new. During a discussion with the theologian Nicodemus, Jesus described this way of relating to God. He told Nicodemus that "no one can see the kingdom of God without being born from above." Nicodemus responded: "How can anyone be born after having grown old? Can one enter a second time into the mother's womb and be born?" (John 3:4). Jesus did not negate Nicodemus's reference to a mother's womb; he simply informed him that it was the womb of God that he needed to enter. Jesus said: "What is born of flesh is flesh, and what is born of the Spirit is spirit. Do not be astonished that I said to you, 'You must be born from above'" (John 3:6-7).

I suggest that many of us have missed the full meaning of this text. Jesus said that by entering the womb of God we can find freedom from a history we have either created or inherited (the realm of the flesh). Then we can be renewed by the

Spirit. We can declare with the apostle Paul, "Everything old has passed away; see, everything has become new!" (2 Corinthians 5:17). The womb-of-God experience helps us cast off any dysfunction found in our emotions, spirit, psyche, and relationships. It is essential that we also let go of the legacy of historical pain. I am not suggesting that we fail to repair the wrong done in the past. I do contend that we can create a future that is no longer held captive by the past. Our ability to experience reconciliation in its fullness is dependent on being healed from the spiritual, emotional, and psychological injuries that come from our personal, cultural, or family histories.

Although I have suggested that healing produces restfulness, this healing does not happen unless we take action. The purpose of a womb is to prepare one for birth. The idea of the womb of God most certainly suggests birth, a new beginning. For Gary Steele, to whom I referred earlier in this chapter, the deep healing that cleansed his soul from the infection of racism occurred because it seemed imperative to take some action. After becoming a Christian, and even more so after completing seminary, he "felt lousy about being a racist." He also felt powerless to change. One day he told his story to the late Bill Leslie. This seasoned urban pastor challenged Gary by asking, "How are you using your past painful experiences for Jesus Christ?" Gary was taken aback by the question; he had been preoccupied with how terrible it felt to be a racist. Upon further reflection, he found the honesty of Bill Leslie's statement to be a source of hope. Gary discovered that action was essential for reconciliation even if awkward initially.

Shortly thereafter, Gary encountered a Native American. Instead of reacting negatively, remaining content to think through the experience conceptually, or avoiding the situation altogether, he asked, "Can we please talk?" The man responded, "I don't talk to white people." Gary reiterated his desire to have a conversation because he felt that he desperately needed his help. This time the man agreed. Gary told his story and detailed his racism. Their conversation became a therapeutic moment for both men and began a friendship.[12] Gary Steele moved out of his comfort zone of analysis, took action, and discovered the humanity of someone he previously would have discounted. He also rediscovered his own identity. Reconciliation had begun.

The womb of God is the place of healing. Wherever we may be in life, we can enter the safe, secure presence of God. The invitation to be born from above is a comforting call to accept God's healing. Our bruised identities and our scarred pasts can receive the healing balm of divine love in the womb of God. Reconciled to God *and ourselves,* we can step back into life, reborn from above. Lasting reconciliation across the dividing walls of hostility will elude us if we do not experience a deep personal and societal healing.

A Community of the Reconciled

In order to sustain healing and reconciled relationships, we must bring into being a new way of relating to one another. I once again return to the example of a broken marriage. When a couple's relationship has been violated, both people must take responsibility to initiate a process of reconciliation. This is followed by forgiveness and some form of repairing the wrong incurred. After this has been accomplished, a deep pain may remain, and further healing must be sought. Yet this is not enough. Because the old way of interacting resulted in a broken marriage, a new way of relating as wife and husband must be created that can sustain the reconciled relationship. In order to carry out our efforts to create a harmonious society, we must formulate a way of interacting that is free from all hints of injustice and division.

A first step in transforming the patterns of relationships as they presently exist in society is to give birth to a community of the reconciled. In this smaller setting, whether it be a local congregation or another form of intentional community, we can perfect ways of relating that in turn can be introduced into larger society. This fellowship of unity will be guided by new rules. We will need to define how reconciled people should relate to one another. We all can have a role in designing this new way of coming together. For example, in a community of the reconciled, gender equality would be pursued and modeled. Girls and boys could observe new ways of expressing equality in the lives of men and women. The rules of gender relationships can be changed, and we can also reshape the rules governing other spheres of relating.

We can begin by discovering what is best about our relationships as they now exist. What are the life-giving dynamics in our relationships? Next we might imagine the new possibilities. What are our dreams and heart-cries telling us about the ideal ways of relating to one another? [13] Also, what are the biblical images of how we can live together?[14] After collecting our thoughts about the best of our present reality, our visions for the future, and the biblical models, we need to use these ideas to engage in dialogue. If in the process of interchange a consensus begins to emerge, we will have a notion about the essence of our shared community. After we agree upon a vision of a reconciled community, we must begin to construct it.

As we transform unreconciled relationships into a community of reconciled people, we must apply our learnings from the community setting to the society as a whole. If we can attain reconciled social, economic, and political arrangements, our whole way of relating in society can change in one generation. We can begin to end racism, sexism, classism, and other forms of bigotry by raising a new generation of people who value one another as human brothers and sisters. We are not imprisoned by history, doomed to repeat the behaviors

of our ancestors. We can create a future that follows a new
blueprint for human interaction and social groupings.

Living in the Tension

Sometimes we find common ground elusive on certain
issues. This is a challenge for a community of the reconciled.
I participated in a reconciliation service after the O. J. Simpson verdicts were announced. The gathering was supported
and attended by a wide range of Christians. The focus of the
event was to encourage a process of healing around issues of
race and domestic abuse. While the service effectively initiated this discussion, two speakers went off on tangents. One
person made comments supporting a hierarchical relationship in marriage. Another individual spoke about reconciliation with homosexuals. Neither comment related directly to
the issue of healing in the wake of the O. J. Simpson verdicts.
Though these interjections may have been inappropriate and
though some may have felt very uncomfortable about one or
both of the comments, no one left the service. Everyone
remained in the tension because of a shared commitment to
Jesus Christ and to reconciliation.

Part of living in a reconciled community is the ability to
live in the tension. Living in the tension means agreeing to
disagree and respecting each other as people of faith while
doing the best we can to comprehend complex issues. People
who claim the name of Christ are on both sides of issues like
political affiliation, sexual orientation, capital punishment,
abortion, euthanasia, and interfaith involvement. If we can
live in the tension of being on opposites sides of certain issues
and still consider each other sisters and brothers, we will
remain reconciled.

Tony and Peggy Campolo are a husband and wife who
disagree on whether practicing homosexuals can be Christians.[15] Both believe that the Bible supports their perspective.
Tony feels that although we must not condemn people with

a homosexual orientation, Scripture supports sexual relationships only in the context of monogamous heterosexual
marriage. Peggy believes that the Bible does not condemn
sexual relationships for homosexuals who "live out the kind
of covenant that biblically prescribed marriage requires."[16]
The Campolos have remained married and have not de-
nounced each other's faith despite their lack of agreement on
this issue. Tony Campolo comments:

> I suggest that Peggy and I are modeling what Christian
> marriage is all about. Ours is a marriage in which we
> respect each other's opinions and defend each other's
> right to be a person with his or her own ideas and
> beliefs. . . . I believe what is going on between Peggy and
> me, as we differ from each other on this crucial culture-
> war issue, is modeling in a personal way what the
> church needs to embrace—the fact that serious differ-
> ences do not necessitate a divorce. . . . On many issues,
> Christians must learn that on this side of glory there
> may not be resolutions to those dramatically opposed
> beliefs that divide us. We must learn to live in unity
> while affirming our individual right to differ.[17]

An example of how a congregation has actualized this
"living in unity" is described in a World Vision case study
based on a composite account of two Southern California
congregations exploring responses to the issue of abortion.
Members at "Community Church of Anytown, USA" represented three perspectives on abortion:

> "I am definitely Pro-Life."
> "It is such a complex issue, but I am unquestioningly
> Pro-Choice."
> "I don't know what I believe. I am so sure that an
> unborn child is loved by God in the same way a born
> child is, but my daughter who is a born-again Chris-
> tian made what I am convinced was a prayerful deci-
> sion to abort a 3-month-old baby (or fetus) who would

> have been born with horrible mental and physical prob-
> lems and would maybe have only lived for a week."

The congregation was approximately 40 percent pro-life, 40 percent pro-choice, and 20 percent undecided. The members were nearly evenly divided by political party affiliation. According to people on both sides, "it seems that it is absolutely impossible for the two sides of the abortion issue to find common ground." Then the congregation started a center for homeless women and children. People from both sides of the abortion issue incarnated God's love for individuals and families who had been hurt by life's circumstances. At the same time, by "working together they [found] friendships with each other in ways that [seemed] impossible for people on opposite sides of the abortion issue to have."[18]

The two previous examples suggest that community calls us to endure in the midst of difficult situations. There are limits to our ability to live in tension and remain a community of the reconciled. We cannot accept any form of oppression or dehumanization. For instance, we could not live in the tension around the issue of slavery. The community of the reconciled will have to struggle to define the limits of this tension. Yet on many issues we can coexist in the midst of a lack of corporate clarity. We can move forward in the direction of healing and create a new community.

The peace of God awaits us if we choose to enter the womb of God. There we find restored identity, revived emotion, renewed energy, and resurrected hope. Then we can advance toward discovering a new way of relating in a community of the reconciled. It is the community of Jesus Christ: where all are welcome at the table of fellowship; where all voices and viewpoints are treasured; where each person is fluent in the experiences of others. We have a long way to travel down the road of reconciliation before we arrive at such a desired state of togetherness. So we must engage in the process of costly reconciliation that calls us to take responsibility, pursue forgiveness, repair wrongs, heal our souls, and create a new way of relating.

Questions for Discussion

1. How would you define *identity*? Do you agree with the author that a crisis of identity is at the root of many of our social problems? If so, cite some examples. If not, what do you think is the root problem and why?

2. Do you believe that dysfunction can be passed on from generation to generation in a society? If so, describe cases where you believe this has occurred.

3. Do you believe that injustice has had an impact on you personally—physically, emotionally, psychologically, spiritually? Share any of these that you feel comfortable acknowledging.

4. When you hear the phrase "womb of God," what thoughts come to mind? Do you believe that God can heal our inner beings? If so, why do you believe this? If not, why are you unable to accept this idea?

5. How can we heal the effects of each of these injustices: homophobia, classism, anti-Semitism, sexism, nationalism, racism? Are there other injustices you would add to the list? Be sure to address all sides of the situation: the positions of victims, perpetrators, bystanders, and those who have inherited injustice, for example.

6. What are some strategies for creating a new way of relating across the divide of race, gender, class, nation, culture, and religion? Do you believe it is possible to develop a community of the reconciled in some form? Explain your answer. Can you live in the tension? What are your limits?

7. Chapters 7–9 described a process of reconciliation that included the following: taking responsibility, pursuing forgiveness, repairing wrongs, healing the soul, and creating a new way of relating. Should other steps be included? What are they, and why are they important? What, in your opinion, are the costs of pursuing the process of reconciliation? What needs to happen if Christians are to move forward in practicing reconciliation?

Part IV

A Costly Practice

10

Epilogue

In the preceding pages, I have tried to paint a fresh portrait of reconciliation. I have noted many of the costly problems facing us, both in society and in the church, as a result of disregard for or cheap attempts at reconciliation. I have lifted up the costly proclamation of reconciliation that was the defining message of Jesus and the first-century church. I suggested that this proclamation needs to be evident in our attitudes, beliefs, and actions. Then I described the costly process of moving toward wholeness. The process of reconciliation advances when we take responsibility, participate in forgiveness, repair wrongs, heal our souls, and create new ways of relating to each other. All that remains is to step out into the midst of a polarized world and pursue the work of restitching the patchwork of human relationships. Reconciliation has to be acted on to be of any value. Moving forward on the journey that leads to unity means taking risks. The practice of reconciliation is costly.

Two years after Dietrich Bonhoeffer published his book *The Cost of Discipleship*, he left Germany intent on spending a year or so in the United States. Bonhoeffer's purpose for the trip was to communicate with Christians outside of Germany, to tell the real story of the danger posed by the Nazis. He also would teach, reflect, and rest while in the United

States. But Bonhoeffer began to have second thoughts in the
final days before he left. Church leaders in Germany were
continuing to bow to the demands of the Nazi government,
and many were stating their support for Hitler's policies.
These church leaders proclaimed that they would commit "to
join fully and devotedly in the Führer's national political
constructive work. . . . In the national sphere of life there must
be a serious and responsible racial policy of maintaining the
purity of the nation."[1]

Despite his concerns, Bonhoeffer set sail for the United
States. Upon his arrival, however, his reservations grew
stronger. He was welcomed with open arms by Americans
who believed they were rescuing him from the dangers of
Germany. Dietrich Bonhoeffer stayed in the United States
less than two months. In a letter to Reinhold Neibuhr he
explained his decision to return to Germany: "I have made a
mistake in coming to America. I must live through this
difficult period of our national history with the Christian
people of Germany. I will have no right to participate in the
reconstruction of Christian life in Germany after the war if I
do not share the trials of this time with my people."[2]

Bonhoeffer's decision to return to Germany was a turning
point in his leadership. It demonstrated the strength of his
commitment to freedom. He chose the road of costly grace.
He practiced what he preached. Bonhoeffer had written in
The Cost of Discipleship that "when Christ calls a man, he bids
him come and die."[3] By choosing to return to Germany, he
died to the reasonable desire for rest and safety. He let go of
his own desires so that he could embrace God's desire. Like
Dietrich Bonhoeffer, we may be tempted to choose a reasonable path of less resistance. The cost of practicing reconciliation may mean that we die to our dreams and goals, as well
as to our desire to live a "normal" life. Reconciliation calls us
to choose the costly practice of bringing people together. In
the final pages of this book, I offer brief glimpses of a few of

the roles that must be embodied in the practice of reconciliation. Our troubled times ask us to become artisans of reconciliation,[4] visionary activists,[5] serious empathics, courageous
prophets, patient mediators, and compassionate advocates.[6]

Artisans of Reconciliation

Our faith expresses itself through reconciliation with God,
ourselves, and others. Reconciliation *is* God's one-item
agenda. Given this understanding, the image of an artisan of
reconciliation is a compelling one. An artisan is an individual
who becomes exceptionally accomplished at a skill by committing his or her life to developing a craft. An artisan could
be a person who spends his or her entire life perfecting the
nuances of carving beautiful wood furniture. Each turn of the
blade is mastered through much discipline and diligence. So
as artisans of reconciliation, we devote our lives to becoming
more skilled at the art of relational bridge building. We
delight at the opportunity to sharpen our diplomatic skills in
the drama of human social intercourse. We are faithful in
developing our God-given reconciling gifts within the context of separation and alienation. The artisan of reconciliation
is able to walk with grace "through a minefield of so many
subtle discriminations."[7] The world needs artisans who can
propel the process of reconciliation forward. As artisans of
reconciliation we are constantly honing our ability to take
responsibility, encourage forgiveness, repair wrongs, heal
souls, and create new ways of relating.

Visionary Activists

In order to use our reconciling gifts, we will need to be
both visionaries and activists. As visionaries, we learn to
recognize separation and oppression while we develop our
comprehension of the multiple causes of injustice. Further,
we seek to understand how injustice produces long-term
oppression. Most important, we are able to understand what

creates a just society. We know how many strokes of the brush are necessary to paint the perfect picture on the canvas of humanity. Robert Kennedy's often-repeated paraphrase of the words of George Bernard Shaw captures the quintessence of the visionary: "Some [people] see things as they are, and say why; I dream of things that never were, and say why not?"[8] These visions of reconciliation and social justice spring forth from a faith that is "the assurance of things hoped for, the conviction of things not seen" (Hebrews 11:1). As ambassadors of unity we develop, in theologian Amos Wilder's words, a "visionary capacity at least as potent as that of the prevailing secular dreams and idolatries."[9] We also embrace the role of the activist by devising and executing processes for moving away from the way things are and toward the way they should be. The reconciler is so caught up in the genuine belief that conditions actually can improve that he or she inspires others to labor for transformation.

Serious Empathics

In addition to being visionary activists, we also are serious empathics. If you have watched the television show *Star Trek: The Next Generation*, then you are familiar with the character Counselor Troi, counselor on the spaceship the *Starship Enterprise*. What makes her particularly adept at this challenging assignment is that she comes from a planet whose inhabitants have highly developed extrasensory abilities. This empathic ability allows her not only to perceive the psychological state of coworkers but also to sense the emotions of potential adversaries. Counselor Troi is able to experience, viscerally, the feelings of others.

In much the same way, we must perceive the splits in society and feel deeply the pain caused by such division. Sexism, classism, and racism are experienced as events. Where we do not have firsthand experience, we can enter into these occurrences through the stories told by the victims of prejudice. We learn to feel the torment of desperation and alienation. Then we lament these relational ruptures. Such deep empathy leads us to respond with greater seriousness. We are earnest about healing brokenness because we experience the agony of unreconciled relationships.

Courageous Prophets

Because the reconciler takes seriously the chasm in society, he or she feels compelled to announce publicly that division exists. Racism, classism, sexism, anti-Semitism, homophobia, and other forms of bigotry cannot remain hidden. They must be brought out into the light. It is the role of the reconciler to accomplish this. Such prophetic announcements risk a negative response from those benefiting from the status quo. Professor Doris Donnelly reminds us that "we run the risk of peeving the power brokers who have much to lose if their unilateral power base is brought into question. But that is precisely what the reconciler is willing to do, unpopular as the task is."[10] The system that perpetuates injustice and division in society will attempt to undermine people who take action on a vision for reconciliation and social justice. Although the struggle is against a system of evil, injustice often wears the cloak of flesh and blood. The faith-inspired reconciler must learn to recognize people who cannot be trusted, as well as systems that are unjust.

Efforts to promote unity are considered a direct threat by the guardians of unjust systems. In their minds these efforts cannot be allowed to succeed, or the power of the status quo is jeopardized. For this reason, the powers that be had Jesus crucified and the apostle Paul beheaded. Dietrich Bonhoeffer's commitment to costly grace and his acceptance of Christ's call to come and die led to his execution by the Nazi government at the age of thirty-nine. The role of the courageous prophet may entail great cost. Yet our hope and strength emerge out of our own experience of reconciliation with God.

Whatever the inherent risk, the knowledge that God reached
out and loved us when we felt alienated propels us to seek
peace and wholeness for our world.

Patient Mediators

Notwithstanding the potential for persecution, the reconciler patiently stands in the middle of chaos proclaiming the
message of peace. We intentionally place ourselves in settings of separation and strife. It is only when we are in the
midst of division that we can jump-start the process of reconciliation. Our witness loses its credibility if we attempt to
build bridges from afar. This is why Dietrich Bonhoeffer had
to return to Germany. He could not talk about reconciliation
from a place of safety, far away from the struggle. He had to
be at the heart of the challenging experience to be able to have
an impact on the outcome. Also by positioning ourselves at
the center of situations of separation, we are better able to
watch for catalytic moments that might propel reconciliation.
Sometimes the slightest shift in posture allows us to facilitate
a coming together. We cannot see these opportunities for
concord from a distance. Therefore, the intermediary must
have patience and not leave the core of chaos too soon. The
patient mediator believes that reconciliation is always possible at some level. We celebrate any move toward harmony.

Compassionate Advocates

Although the role of mediator implies intercession without taking sides, in situations where we can clearly delineate
victims and victimizers, there are limits to our patience with
oppressors. When reconciliation efforts are at a standstill and
people are being victimized, we step in and press for their
liberation. We take action against systems of injustice and the
perpetrators of oppression. This may also mean working in
ministries of compassion as direct service providers. If we
sell out justice by taking an "impartial" role, we will hear the

voice of Jesus crying out, "I was hungry and you gave me no food, I was thirsty and you gave me nothing to drink, I was a stranger and you did not welcome me, naked and you did not give me clothing, sick and in prison and you did not visit me" (Matthew 25:35-36). Repairing the wrong of injustice through merciful action moves us toward reconciliation. As compassionate advocates, we may work for reconciliation in many ways—serving at homeless shelters, building houses in impoverished areas, buying back stolen lands. We cannot stand idly by as the cleavage widens between the powerful and powerless in society. Also we are still called to work for reconciliation even when faced with apparent irreconcilable differences. For when the mending of broken relationships does not take place, pain festers. In the absence of unity, we can show compassion through acts of healing. As reconcilers, we advocate compassion when all other efforts are floundering.

Now Is the Time!

Right after the apostle Paul's eloquent declaration, in 2 Corinthians 5:16-21, that followers of Jesus Christ were called to be ambassadors of reconciliation, he wrote, "Now is the acceptable time . . . now is the day of salvation!" (6:2). The time to begin our efforts toward reconciliation is now! Let us never become comfortable with sexist attitudes, class-based societies, racially segregated congregations, and the idea of denominationalism, because now is the time for reconciliation. Let us not become discouraged in the face of ethnic cleansing, religious bigotry, neo-Nazism, entrenched racism, or anything else that polarizes the human family, because now is the time for reconciliation. In a world estranged from itself, now is the time for us to hear the call, accept the challenge, stand up, and step forward as God's artisans of reconciliation. Reconciliation is a long-term process. It occurs on God's timetable. We must be realistic and prepared for a lifelong journey. Yet it is a journey worth taking. Although costly reconciliation is our greatest challenge, it is our only hope! And our hope is like none other, because we serve a God who took a carpenter-turned-prophet named Jesus, lying dead in a borrowed tomb, and raised him up to life, validating forever the message of reconciliation and love.

Notes

Introduction

1. The Bibliography for Reconcilers in this volume gives an idea of the range of these titles. For examples of books on racial reconciliation coauthored by an African American male and a white male, see John Perkins and Thomas A. Tarrants III, *He's My Brother: Former Racial Foes Offer Strategy for Reconciliation* (Grand Rapids, Mich.: Chosen Books, 1994); Spencer Perkins and Chris Rice, *More than Equals: Racial Healing for the Sake of the Gospel* (Downers Grove, Ill.: InterVarsity Press, 1993); and Raleigh Washington and Glen Kehrein, *Breaking Down Walls: A Model for Reconciliation in an Age of Racial Strife* (Chicago: Moody Press, 1993).

2. Dietrich Bonhoeffer, *The Cost of Discipleship* (1937; reprint, New York: Simon and Schuster, 1995), 44, 45.

3. Ibid., 45.

4. See Robert J. Schreiter, *Reconciliation: Mission and Ministry in a Changing Social Order* (Maryknoll, N.Y.: Orbis Books, 1992), 18-27.

5. Curtiss Paul DeYoung, *Coming Together: The Bible's Message in an Age of Diversity* (Valley Forge, Pa.: Judson Press, 1995).

6. The results of these interviews can be found in Curtiss

Paul DeYoung, *Milwaukee's Faith Community Speaks* (Milwaukee: Social Development Commission, 1991).

Chapter 1

1. Eldin Villafañe, *Seek the Peace of the City: Reflections on Urban Ministry* (Grand Rapids, Mich.: Eerdmans, 1995), 61.

2. William Pannell, *The Coming Race Wars? A Cry for Reconciliation* (Grand Rapids, Mich.: Zondervan, 1993).

3. Roberto W. Pazmiño, "Double Dutch: Reflections of an Hispanic North American on Multicultural Religious Education," in *Voces: Voices from the Hispanic Church*, ed. Justo L. González (Nashville: Abingdon, 1992), 139-40.

4. James Earl Massey, *Concerning Christian Unity: A Study of the Relational Imperative of Agape Love* (Anderson, Ind.: Warner Press, 1979), 58.

5. C. Eric Lincoln, *Coming through the Fire: Surviving Race and Place in America* (Durham, N.C.: Duke University Press, 1996), 14.

6. Elaine Storkey, *What's Right with Feminism* (Grand Rapids, Mich.: Eerdmans, 1985), 162.

7. See Perkins and Rice, 23-31.

8. While Martin Luther King Jr. was talking about a dream, Malcolm X was predicting a nightmare. See James H. Cone, *Martin and Malcolm and America: A Dream or a Nightmare?* (Maryknoll, N.Y.: Orbis Books, 1991).

9. James Newton Poling, *Deliver Us from Evil: Resisting Racial and Gender Oppression* (Minneapolis: Fortress Press, 1996), xvi.

10. Al Miles, "Racism in Hawai'i: Myths and Realities," *Honolulu*, July 1995, 67.

11. For a good discussion of denial, see Paul Kivel, *Uprooting Racism: How White People Can Work for Racial Justice* (Philadelphia: New Society Publishers, 1996), 40-46.

12. Howard Thurman, *The Luminous Darkness: A Personal*

Interpretation of the Anatomy of Segregation and the Ground of Hope (New York: Harper and Row, 1965), 66, 67.

Chapter 2

1. James Earl Massey, "Arrogance Always Limits Us," *Shining Light*, September/October 1987, 5.

2. Tonda S. Clarke, "The Invisible Woman: Plantation Protocol in Contemporary America," *Colors* 4, no. 6 (November–December 1995), 15-16.

3. For a historical perspective on the melting pot in American history and its effect on various groups of people, see Ronald Takaki, *A Different Mirror: A History of Multicultural America* (Boston: Little, Brown, 1993).

4. Jeff King, "The American Indian: The Invisible Man," in Rodney L. Cooper, *We Stand Together: Reconciling Men of Different Color* (Chicago: Moody Press, 1995), 84.

5. Fumitaka Matsuoka, *Out of Silence: Emerging Themes in Asian American Churches* (Cleveland: United Church Press, 1995), 57.

6. Ibid., 48.

7. Story recounted in Thurman, *Luminous Darkness*, 36-37.

8. Malcolm X, *February 1965: The Final Speeches* (New York: Pathfinder, 1992), 27-28.

9. Al Miles, "Reflection: Racism in a Health Care Setting," *Healing Ministry*, January/February 1995, 16.

10. Ibid.

11. Perkins and Rice, 95.

12. Catherine Meeks, "Rage and Reconciliation: Two Sides of the Same Coin," *America's Original Sin: A Study Guide on White Racism* (Washington, D.C.: Sojourners, 1992), 98, 99.

13. Ray Bradbury, *The Illustrated Man* (1951; reprint, Toronto: Bantam Books, 1982), 27-38.

14. Ibid., 29-30.

15. Ibid., 36.

16. Ibid., 38.

17. Quoted in Takaki, 75.

18. Thurman, *Luminous Darkness*, 72, 73.

Chapter 3

1. Arthur Huff Fauset, "Ain't I a Woman?" *America's Original Sin: A Study Guide on White Racism* (Washington, D.C.: Sojourners, 1992), 81.

2. Thurman, *Luminous Darkness*, 60-61.

3. Martin Luther King Jr., *A Testament of Hope: The Essential Writings of Martin Luther King, Jr.* (San Francisco: Harper and Row, 1986), 101.

4. For an expanded discussion of the so-called curses of Cain and Ham, see Cain Hope Felder, "Race, Racism, and the Biblical Narratives," and Charles B. Copher, "The Black Presence in the Old Testament," in *Stony the Road We Trod: African American Biblical Interpretation*, ed. Cain Hope Felder (Minneapolis: Fortress Press, 1991), 129-32, 146-53, and DeYoung, *Coming Together*, 12-13, 122-24.

5. Although there are many Semitic peoples, the term *anti-Semitism* has come to refer to prejudice against Jewish people.

6. Calvin S. Morris, "We, the White People: A History of Oppression," *Sojourners*, November 1987, 19, 20.

7. Dietrich Bonhoeffer, *Letters and Papers from Prison: The Enlarged Edition*, ed. Eberhard Bethge (1953; reprint, New York: Macmillan, 1972), 300.

8. Howard Thurman, *Jesus and the Disinherited* (1949; reprint, Richmond, Ind.: Friends United Press, 1981), 98.

9. Samuel G. Hines, with Joe Allison, *Experience the Power*, rev. ed. (Anderson, Ind.: Warner Press, 1996), 85.

10. Cheryl Sanders, "We Have Nothing to Show the World," *Christianity Today*, October 4, 1993, 23.

11. Gordon W. Allport, *The Nature of Prejudice* (1954; reprint, Reading, Pa.: Addison-Wesley, 1979), 444.

12. Ibid., 454.

13. E. Stanley Jones, *Mahatma Gandhi: An Interpretation* (New York: Abingdon-Cokesbury Press, 1948), 54.

14. Ibid., 55.

15. Malcolm X, *The Autobiography of Malcolm X* (1965; reprint, New York: Ballantine Books, 1973), 241-42.

16. Allport, 456.

17. The Re-Imagining Community, based in Minneapolis, Minn., is the result of the 1993 Re-Imagining Conference. The event, which considered how Christian theology could be understood through the experience of women, produced a great amount of controversy.

18. DeYoung, *Coming Together*, 38-45.

19. Ibid., 38-39.

20. Francisco M. Penning, "A Response to *Coming Together*," September 20, 1995.

21. William Sloane Coffin, *A Passion for the Possible: A Message to U.S. Churches* (Louisville: Westminster/John Knox Press, 1993), 61.

22. Mack King Carter, quoted by David G. Buttrick, "Laughing with the Gospel," in *Sharing Heaven's Music: The Heart of Christian Preaching. Essays in Honor of James Earl Massey*, ed. Barry L. Callen (Nashville: Abingdon, 1995), 126.

23. My response to this question will become evident as you read further in this book. I respond more completely in my book *Coming Together*, 31-63.

Chapter 4

1. Perkins and Rice, 69.

2. Samuel G. Hines, "The Gospel Ministry," in Cheryl J. Sanders, *How Firm a Foundation* (Washington, D.C.: Third Street Church of God, 1990), 74.

3. Harold H. Ditmanson, *Grace in Experience and Theology* (Minneapolis: Augsburg, 1977), 195.

4. Ralph P. Martin, *Reconciliation: A Study of Paul's Theology* (Atlanta: John Knox Press, 1981), 109.

5. Ditmanson, 195.

6. Craig S. Keener, *The IVP Bible Background Commentary: New Testament* (Downers Grove, Ill.: InterVarsity Press, 1993), 423.

7. Some scientists have concluded that all humans come from a common ancestor. See "The Search for Adam and Eve," *Newsweek*, January 11, 1988, 46-53.

8. See DeYoung, *Coming Together,* 1-4.

9. Keener, 544.

10. Ditmanson, 213.

11. John W. V. Smith, *The Quest for Holiness and Unity: A Centennial History of the Church of God (Anderson, Indiana)* (Anderson, Ind.: Warner Press, 1980), 165.

12. Hines, "Gospel Ministry," 77.

13. Fred Burnett, videotaped lecture, Anderson, Ind., December 22, 1989.

14. See Cain Hope Felder, "The Challenges and Implications of Recovering the Afro-Asiatic Identity of Jesus of Nazareth," *BISC Quarterly* 4, no. 1 (1993): 1, 3, 5, 8; and DeYoung, *Coming Together,* 34-36. Our modern society would probably designate Jesus of Nazareth racially as an African American, because at least "one drop" of African blood was running through his veins.

15. See DeYoung, *Coming Together,* 5, 8-11, 34-36.

16. See Pazmiño, 138-39; Virgilio Elizondo, *Galilean Journey: The Mexican-American Promise* (Maryknoll, N.Y.: Orbis Books, 1983), 51; and K. W. Clark, "Galilee," in *The Interpreter's Dictionary of the Bible,* ed. George Arthur Buttrick (Nashville: Abingdon, 1962), 2:344-47.

17. Pazmiño, 139.

18. See DeYoung, *Coming Together,* 5, 136-39.

19. Ibid., 165-68.

20. Hines, "Gospel Ministry," 79.

21. See DeYoung, *Coming Together,* 140-42.

22. Ibid., 28-29.

23. Keener, 528.

24. Doris Donnelly, "Ambassadors of Reconciliation," *Weavings*, January/February 1990, 19-20.

Chapter 5

1. From George Wallace's inauguration speech. See Juan Williams, *Eyes on the Prize: America's Civil Rights Years, 1954–1965* (New York: Viking Penguin, 1987), 183.

2. Joseph E. Lowery, "God Makes the Crooked Places Straight," *Fellowship* 61, no. 7-8 (July/August 1995): 5.

3. Ibid.

4. Jesse Jackson, quoted in John F. Kennedy Jr., "George Wallace," *George*, October/November 1995, 184.

5. The principles in chapters 5 and 6, and the process steps in chapters 7–9, have been derived from the writings, words, and actions of many people.

6. Villafañe, 57-58.

7. Martin Luther King Jr., "Dr. Martin Luther King, Jr. Comments on NAACP Resolution," April 12, 1967, reprint by Clergy and Laymen Concerned about Vietnam, 28, quoted in John J. Ansbro, *Martin Luther King, Jr.: The Making of a Mind* (Maryknoll, N.Y.: Orbis Books, 1982), 264.

8. See Takaki, *A Different Mirror*.

9. Ditmanson, 151, 152.

10. Sethard Beverly, "Farewell to Sam Hines, but Not to His Message and Ministry," *Metro-Voice*, Winter 1994–95, 1.

11. Washington and Kehrein, 235, 240.

12. Kay Cole James, "Separate Vacations," *Christianity Today*, October 4, 1993, 18-19.

13. Samuel G. Hines, quoted in Jane L. Hammond, "Politicians and Poor Pray Together," *Vital Christianity*, January 30, 1983, 24.

14. Ibid., 23, 24.

Chapter 6

1. Nicholas C. Cooper-Lewter and Henry H. Mitchell, *Soul Theology: The Heart of American Black Culture* (San Francisco: Harper and Row, 1986), 101.

2. Martin Luther King Jr., "Remaining Awake through a Great Revolution," in *A Testament of Hope: The Essential Writings of Martin Luther King, Jr.*, ed. James Melvin Washington (San Francisco: Harper and Row, 1986), 269.

3. For a discussion of the role of liberation in the Bible and the Christian faith see DeYoung, *Coming Together*, 91-116.

4. See Schreiter, 1-25.

5. Desmond M. Tutu, "Allies of God." *Weavings*, January/February 1990, 41-42.

6. J. Deotis Roberts, *Liberation and Reconciliation: A Black Theology* (1971; rev. ed., Maryknoll, N.Y.: Orbis Books, 1994), ix.

7. Máiread Maguire, interview by Shelley Anderson and Paula Green, "Reconciliation: Having the Courage to Heal," in Marie-Pierre Bovy, Hildegard Goss-Mayr, Máiread Maguire, and Sulak Sivaraksa, *Reconciliation: Reflections on the Occasion of the 75th Anniversary of the International Fellowship of Reconciliation* (Alkmaar, The Netherlands: International Fellowship of Reconciliation, 1994), 18.

8. DeYoung, *Coming Together*, 177-80. See also the section "Multicultural Competence" in Kivel, 205.

9. DeYoung, *Coming Together*, 174.

10. A good example of this type of history is Takaki, *A Different Mirror*. For a way of studying the Bible from a multicultural perspective see DeYoung, *Coming Together*, 79-82.

11. Eric H. F. Law, *The Wolf Shall Dwell with the Lamb: A Spirituality for Leadership in a Multicultural Community* (St. Louis: Chalice Press, 1993), 79-88.

12. Al Miles expands on the concept of the limits in understanding another's experience when he writes in "Racism in

Hawai'i," 44: "I'm always suspicious of any white person who claims to fully understand. . . . It's been my experience that most whites don't have a clue as to what racism feels like on a deep personal level. Many whites are intellectually and morally sensitive to the problem. Some have even suffered a degree of discrimination. But their race is treated as superior, not placed in an inferior position like many other racial groups. When one comes from a position of power and superiority, as do whites, it is nearly impossible to internalize the feelings of those who have lived under constant oppression simply because of their racial heritage. And besides, who would want to internalize these feelings? Racism feels awful."

13. Meeks, 98-99.

Chapter 7

1. Maguire, 7.

2. "His Mission for Unity," *Minneapolis Star Tribune*, August 16, 1995, 2A.

3. Billy Graham, "Racism and the Evangelical Church," *Christianity Today*, October 4, 1993, 27.

4. Morris, 21.

5. Karen McKinney, "The Road to Understanding: A Seminar Curriculum for Unlearning Racism," paper presented in Experiential Education 694 at Mankato State University, Mankato, Minn., March 1995, 22-24.

6. Samuel G. Hines, quoted in "Church Leaders Work for Racial Reconciliation," *Christianity Today*, November 8, 1985, 69, 70.

7. Unidentified woman, quoted in Howard Thurman, *Disciplines of the Spirit* (1963; 2d ed., Richmond, Ind.: Friends United Press, 1987), 117.

8. Bonhoeffer, *Letters and Papers from Prison*, 17.

Chapter 8

1. Violette Nyirarukundo, conversation with author, St. Paul, Minn., June 14, 1996. Also around the table that day were Paul and Lisa Sinclair and Robin Bell.

2. Lincoln, 157.

3. See Rodney L. Cooper, *We Stand Together: Reconciling Men of Different Color* (Chicago: Moody Press, 1995), 55-56.

4. Gene Knudsen Hoffman, *No Royal Road to Reconciliation: Reflections on Trauma and Some Psychological and Spiritual Possibilities It Brings to Reconciliation* (Alkmaar, The Netherlands: International Fellowship of Reconciliation, 1994), 35.

5. Charles Villa-Vicencio, "A Cycle of Healing: South Africa Grapples with Reconciliation," *Sojourners*, July-August 1996, 10.

6. Takaki, *A Different Mirror*.

7. DeYoung, *Coming Together*, 38-45.

8. Ibid., 47-62.

9. Penning, "Response." The idea of a Galilean *Jíbaro* Jesus comes from Orlando Costas, who speaks of Jesus in solidarity with the *jibaros* (Puerto Rican peasants). See Orlando Costas, "Liberation Theologies in the Americas: Common Journeys and Mutual Challenges," in *Yearning to Breathe Free: Liberation Theologies in the United States*, ed. Mar Peter-Raoul, Linda Rennie Forcey, and Robert Frederick Hunter Jr. (Maryknoll, N.Y.: Orbis Books, 1990), 42-43. Also see DeYoung, *Coming Together*, 51-52.

10. See Lincoln, 43.

11. Naim Ateek, quoted in Timothy C. Morgan, "Jerusalem's Living Stones," *Christianity Today*, May 20, 1996, 65.

12. Jim Wallis, *The Soul of Politics: A Practical and Prophetic Vision for Change* (New York: New Press; Maryknoll, N.Y.: Orbis Books, 1994), 181, 183.

13. For an example of urban-suburban church partnerships see John Perkins, *Resurrecting Hope: Powerful Stories of*

How God Is Moving to Reach Our Cities (Ventura, Calif.: Regal Books, 1995), 39-50.

14. Winona LaDuke, "Once and Future Harvests," *Sojourners*, September–October, 1993, 1 (on-line edition).

15. Amos Niven Wilder, *Theopoetic: Theology and the Religious Imagination* (Philadelphia: Fortress Press, 1976), 27.

16. Community members served as full-time volunteers at Covenant House, a shelter for runaway and homeless youth.

Chapter 9

1. Maguire, 15.

2. Gary Steele, interview by author, Minneapolis, Minn., August 9, 1996.

3. Nicholas C. Cooper-Lewter, "The Making of the African-American Mind and the Need for Soul Therapy," lecture at Diggs Gallery, Winston-Salem, N.C., March 10, 1994. See numerous examples in Takaki, *A Different Mirror.*

4. See DeYoung, *Coming Together,* 105-9.

5. Thomas Jefferson, *Notes on the State of Virginia* (New York, 1861), 155, quoted in Takaki, 70.

6. See Poling, 3-19. He alludes to such effects, even calling one slave owner a "serial rapist."

7. Knudsen Hoffman, 26-27.

8. Nicholas Cooper-Lewter, "Keep on Rollin' Along: The Temptations and Soul Therapy," *Black Sacred Music: A Journal of Theomusicology* 6, no. 1 (Spring 1992): 218-23. See also Jon Michael Spencer, *Theological Music: Introduction to Theomusicology* (New York: Greenwood Press, 1991), 7, 44-45.

9. Cooper-Lewter, "Making of the African-American Mind."

10. Lincoln, 98.

11. I have heard my friend Rev. Mitchell Bettis tell this story a number of times.

12. Steele, interview.

13. David L. Cooperrider and Suresh Srivastva, "Appreciative

Inquiry in Organizational Life," *Research in Organizational Change and Development* 1 (1987): 129-69.

14. See DeYoung, *Coming Together*, 153-85.

15. Tony Campolo, *Can Mainline Denominations Make a Comeback?* (Valley Forge, Pa.: Judson Press, 1995), 94-98.

16. Ibid., 94.

17. Ibid., 97, 98.

18. "An Enduring Theme for the Ministry of World Vision: Reconciliation—'Living Document' Prepared for Ongoing Discussion," World Vision United States Policy Formation Committee, Draft #4, September 3, 1993, 10.

Chapter 10

1. Edwin Robertson, *The Shame and the Sacrifice: The Life and Martyrdom of Dietrich Bonhoeffer* (New York: Collier Books, Macmillan, 1988), 170.

2. Ibid., 172.

3. Bonhoeffer, *Cost of Discipleship*, 89.

4. See *Christian Community Bible*, 2d ed. (Quezon City; Makati; Manila, Philippines: Claretian Publications, Saint Paul Publications, Divine Word Publications, 1988), 369. Also see DeYoung, *Coming Together*, 183-88.

5. See DeYoung, *Coming Together*, 186-87.

6. Some of these roles are adapted from Donnelly, 18-29.

7. Henry H. Mitchell's description of James Earl Massey in Henry H. Mitchell, "An Interview with James Earl Massey: Veteran Inhabitant of the World We Hope For," in *Sharing Heaven's Music: The Heart of Christian Preaching. Essays in Honor of James Earl Massey*, ed. Barry L. Callen (Nashville: Abingdon, 1995), 218.

8. Jules Witcover, *85 Days: The Last Campaign of Robert Kennedy* (New York: William Morrow, 1988), 8.

9. Wilder, 26.

10. Donnelly, 27.

A Bibliography for Reconcilers

Allport, Gordon W. *The Nature of Prejudice*. 1954. Reprint, Reading, Pa.: Addison-Wesley, 1979.

America's Original Sin: A Study Guide on White Racism. Washington, D.C.: Sojourners, 1992.

Barndt, Joseph. *Dismantling Racism: The Continuing Challenge to White America*. Minneapolis: Augsburg, 1991.

Bonhoeffer, Dietrich. *The Cost of Discipleship*. 1937. Reprint, New York: Simon and Schuster, 1995.

———. *Letters and Papers from Prison: The Enlarged Edition*, ed. Eberhard Bethge. 1953. Reprint, New York: Macmillan, 1972.

———. *Life Together*. New York: Harper and Row, 1954.

Bovy, Marie-Pierre, Hildegard Goss-Mayr, Máiread Maguire, and Sulak Sivaraksa. *Reconciliation: Reflections on the Occasion of the 75th Anniversary of the International Fellowship of Reconciliation*. Alkmaar, The Netherlands: International Fellowship of Reconciliation, 1994.

Callen, Barry L., ed. *Sharing Heaven's Music: The Heart of Christian Preaching. Essays in Honor of James Earl Massey*. Nashville: Abingdon, 1995.

Coffin, William Sloane. *A Passion for the Possible: A Message to U.S. Churches*. Louisville: Westminster/John Knox Press, 1993.

Collum, Danny Duncan. *Black and White Together: The Search for Common Ground*. Maryknoll, N.Y.: Orbis Books, 1996.

Cone, James H. *Martin and Malcolm and America: A Dream or a Nightmare*. Maryknoll, N.Y.: Orbis Books, 1991.

Cooper, Rodney L. *We Stand Together: Reconciling Men of Different Color.* Chicago: Moody Press, 1995.

Cooper-Lewter, Nicholas C., and Henry H. Mitchell. *Soul Theology: The Heart of American Black Culture.* San Francisco: Harper and Row, 1986.

Daloz, Laurent A. Parks, et al. *Common Fire: Lives of Commitment in a Complex World.* Boston: Beacon Press, 1996.

Dayton, Donald W. *Discovering an Evangelical Heritage.* Peabody, Mass.: Hendrickson Publishers, 1976.

Deats, Richard, ed. *Ambassador of Reconciliation: A Muriel Lester Reader.* Philadelphia: New Society Publishers, 1991.

DeYoung, Curtiss Paul. *Coming Together: The Bible's Message in an Age of Diversity.* Valley Forge, Pa.: Judson Press, 1995.

Ditmanson, Harold H. *Grace in Experience and Theology.* Minneapolis: Augsburg, 1977.

Erskine, Noel Leo. *King among the Theologians.* Cleveland: Pilgrim Press, 1994.

Felder, Cain Hope. *Troubling Biblical Waters: Race, Class and Family.* Maryknoll, N.Y.: Orbis Books, 1989.

———, ed. *Stony the Road We Trod: African American Biblical Interpretation.* Minneapolis: Fortress Press, 1991.

González, Justo L. *Out of Every Tribe and Nation: Christian Theology at the Ethnic Roundtable.* Nashville: Abingdon, 1992.

———, ed. *Voces: Voices from the Hispanic Church.* Nashville: Abingdon, 1992.

———, and Catherine Gunsalus González. *Liberation Preaching: The Pulpit and the Oppressed.* Nashville: Abingdon, 1980.

Gordon, Wayne L. *Real Hope in Chicago.* Grand Rapids, Mich.: Zondervan, 1995.

Hacker, Andrew. *Two Nations: Black and White, Separate, Hostile, Unequal.* New York: Charles Scribner's Sons, 1992.

Harkness, Georgia. *The Ministry of Reconciliation.* Nashville: Abingdon, 1971.

Hines, Samuel G. *Experience the Power.* Rev. ed. Anderson, Ind.: Warner Press, 1996.

Jones, E. Stanley. *The Reconstruction of the Church—On What Pattern?* Nashville: Abingdon, 1970.

Kim, Young-IL, ed. *Knowledge, Attitude, and Experience: Ministry in the Cross-Cultural Context.* Nashville: Abingdon, 1992.

King, Martin Luther Jr. *A Testament of Hope: The Essential Writings of Martin Luther King, Jr.* San Francisco: Harper and Row, 1986.

Kivel, Paul. *Uprooting Racism: How White People Can Work for Racial Justice.* Philadelphia: New Society Publishers, 1996.

Knudsen Hoffman, Gene. *No Royal Road to Reconciliation: Reflections on Trauma and Some Psychological and Spiritual Possibilities It Brings to Reconciliation.* Alkmaar, The Netherlands: International Fellowship of Reconciliation, 1994.

———. *Ways Out: The Book of Changes for Peace.* Santa Barbara, Calif.: John Daniel, 1988.

Law, Eric H. F. *The Wolf Shall Dwell with the Lamb: A Spirituality for Leadership in a Multicultural·Community.* St. Louis: Chalice Press, 1993.

Leonard, Juanita Evans. *Called to Minister, Empowered to Serve: Women in Ministry.* Anderson, Ind.: Warner Press, 1989.

Lincoln, C. Eric. *Coming through the Fire: Surviving Race and Place in America* (Durham, N.C.: Duke University Press, 1996).

Martin, Ralph P. *Reconciliation: A Study of Paul's Theology.* Atlanta: John Knox Press, 1981.

Massey, James Earl. *Concerning Christian Unity: A Study of the Relational Imperative of Agape Love.* Anderson, Ind.: Warner Press, 1979.

———. *Spiritual Disciplines: Growth through the Practice of Prayer, Fasting, Dialogue, and Worship.* Grand Rapids, Mich.: Francis Asbury Press, 1985.

Matsuoka, Fumitaka. *Out of Silence: Emerging Themes in Asian American Churches.* Cleveland: United Church Press, 1995.

Menchú, Rigoberta. *I, Rigoberta Menchú: An Indian Woman in Guatemala.* London: Verso, 1984.

Pannell, William. *The Coming Race Wars? A Cry for Reconciliation.* Grand Rapids, Mich.: Zondervan, 1993.

Park, Andrew Sung. *Racial Conflict and Healing: An Asian-American Theological Perspective.* Maryknoll, N.Y.: Orbis Books, 1996.

Perkins, John M. *Beyond Charity: The Call to Christian Community Development.* Grand Rapids, Mich.: Baker Books, 1993.

————, ed. *Restoring At-Risk Communities: Doing It Together and Doing It Right*. Grand Rapids, Mich.: Baker Books, 1995.

————, and Jo Kadlecek. *Resurrecting Hope: Powerful Stories of How God Is Moving to Reach Our Cities*. Ventura, Calif.: Regal Books, 1995.

————, and Thomas A. Tarrants III. *He's My Brother: Former Racial Foes Offer Strategy for Reconciliation*. Grand Rapids, Mich.: Chosen Books, 1994.

Perkins, Spencer, and Chris Rice. *More Than Equals: Racial Healing for the Sake of the Gospel*. Downers Grove, Ill.: InterVarsity Press, 1993.

Poling, James Newton. *Deliver Us from Evil: Resisting Racial and Gender Oppression*. Minneapolis: Fortress Press, 1996.

Peter-Raoul, Mar, Linda Rennie Forcey, and Robert Frederick Hunter Jr., eds. *Yearning to Breathe Free: Liberation Theologies in the United States*. Maryknoll, N.Y.: Orbis Books, 1990.

Reconciliation in Difficult Places: Dealing with Our Deepest Differences. Washington Forum. Monrovia, Calif.: World Vision, 1994.

Roberts, J. Deotis. *Liberation and Reconciliation: A Black Theology*. 1971. Rev. ed., Maryknoll, N.Y.: Orbis Books, 1994.

Sanders, Cheryl J. *Empowerment Ethics for a Liberated People*. Minneapolis: Fortress Press, 1995.

————. *Ministry at the Margins: The Prophetic Mission of Women, Youth and the Poor*. Downers Grove, Ill.: InterVarsity Press, 1997.

————. *Saints in Exile: The Holiness-Pentecostal Experience in African American Religion and Culture*. Oxford: Oxford University Press, 1996.

Schreiter, Robert J. *Reconciliation: Mission and Ministry in a Changing Social Order*. Maryknoll, N.Y.: Orbis Books, 1992.

Shearer, Jody Miller. *Enter the River: Healing Steps from White Privilege toward Racial Reconciliation*. Scottdale, Pa.: Herald Press, 1994.

Storkey, Elaine. *What's Right with Feminism*. Grand Rapids, Mich.: Eerdmans, 1985.

Sugirtharajah, R. S., ed. *Voices from the Margin: Interpreting the Bible in the Third World*. Maryknoll, N.Y.: Orbis Books, 1995.

Takaki, Ronald. *A Different Mirror: A History of Multicultural America.* Boston: Little, Brown, 1993.

Tamez, Elsa. *Bible of the Oppressed.* Maryknoll, N.Y.: Orbis Books, 1982.

Thistlethwaite, Susan Brooks, and Mary Potter Engel, eds. *Lift Every Voice: Constructing Christian Theologies from the Underside.* San Francisco: HarperCollins, 1990.

Thurman, Howard. *Disciplines of the Spirit.* 1963. 2d ed., Richmond, Ind.: Friends United Press, 1987.

————. *Jesus and the Disinherited.* New York: Abingdon-Cokesbury Press, 1949.

————. *The Luminous Darkness: A Personal Interpretation of the Anatomy of Segregation and the Ground of Hope.* New York: Harper and Row, 1965.

————. *The Search for Common Ground.* Richmond, Ind.: Friends United Press, 1971.

Tinker, George E. *Missionary Conquest: The Gospel and Native American Genocide.* Minneapolis: Fortress Press, 1993.

Usry, Glenn, and Craig S. Keener. *Black Man's Religion: Can Christianity be Afrocentric?* Downers Grove, Ill.: InterVarsity Press, 1996.

Villafañe, Eldin. *Seek the Peace of the City: Reflections on Urban Ministry.* Grand Rapids, Mich.: Eerdmans, 1995.

Wallis, Jim. *The Soul of Politics: A Practical and Prophetic Vision for Change.* New York: New Press; Maryknoll, N.Y.: Orbis Books, 1994.

————. *Who Speaks for God? An Alternative to the Religious Right—A New Politics of Compassion, Community, and Civility.* New York: Delacorte Press, 1996.

Washington, Raleigh, and Glen Kehrein. *Breaking Down Walls: A Model for Reconciliation in an Age of Racial Strife.* Chicago: Moody Press, 1993.

West, Cornel. *Race Matters.* Boston: Beacon Press, 1993.

Wilder, Amos Niven. *Theopoetic: Theology and the Religious Imagination.* Philadelphia: Fortress Press, 1976.